White-Collar and Financial Crimes

A CASEBOOK OF FRAUDSTERS, SCAM ARTISTS,
AND CORPORATE THIEVES

Jennifer C. Noble

UNIVERSITY OF CALIFORNIA PRESS

University of California Press
Oakland, California

Library of Congress Cataloging-in-Publication Data

Names: Noble, Jennifer C., author.
Title: White collar and financial crimes : a casebook of fraudsters, scam
    artists, and corporate thieves / Jennifer C. Noble.
Description: Oakland, California : University of California Press, [2021] |
    Includes bibliographical references and index.
Identifiers: LCCN 2020028084 (print) | LCCN 2020028085 (ebook) |
    ISBN 9780520302884 (hardback) | ISBN 9780520302891 (paperback) |
    ISBN 9780520972612 (ebook)
Subjects: LCSH: White collar crimes—United States—Case studies. |
    Commercial crimes—United States—Case studies. | Swindlers and
    swindling—United States—Case studies. | Deceptive advertising—United
    States—Case studies. | Computer crimes—United States—Case studies.
Classification: LCC HV6769 .N63 2021 (print) | LCC HV6769 (ebook) |
    DDC 364.16/80973—dc23
LC record available at https://lccn.loc.gov/2020028084
LC ebook record available at https://lccn.loc.gov/2020028085

Manufactured in the United States of America

24   23   22   21
10   9   8   7   6   5   4   3   2   1

CONTENTS

ACKNOWLEDGMENTS

This work would not have been completed without the dedication, direction, and support of many people. First, thanks to Maura Roessner at University of California Press, who was as excited as I was about this project even before it was a rough outline. Her enthusiasm for this endeavor at every stage kept me excited and mostly on track. At times, it seemed as if the universe was against us, as my timeline ran into campus-closing wildfires and then up against a global pandemic. I appreciate Maura's energetic support and confidence in me more than I can ever express.

I am grateful, too, to all the reviewers who took the time to read the proposal and the manuscript in various stages. Their thoughtful feedback and suggestions were incredibly helpful in shaping this idea into a finished manuscript.

Thanks to real estate agent and broker David Holmes, who checked my understanding and translation of the mortgage process.

Thank you to Dave Hermansen, director of enforcement at the Division of Securities of the Utah Department of Commerce, and Chip Lyon, a financial analyst at the Utah Division of Securities, for your assistance in understanding the investigation and prosecution of Dee Randall.

Many thanks to Cheryl Obermiller, who has been generous with her time and in sharing her experience with my students and with me. I also owe her gratitude for writing an excellent guide for small-business owners on how to avoid embezzlement, which I have had the good fortune to recommend to several people.

I also extend my gratitude to Norman Barbosa, former assistant United States attorney in Seattle and one of the prosecutors in *United States v.*

Roman Seleznev, for sharing his time and expertise as I attempted to summarize and condense this complex cybercrime case into one chapter.

I am thankful for the editing skills of my copyeditor, Steven B. Baker. This book is more readable and accurate due to his hard work. Many heartfelt thanks, also, to copyeditor Amanda Borellis, who agreed to proofread the manuscript, even after I told her that I'd written half of it with footnotes and legal citations. She is a brave soul and an excellent editor.

As always, thanks to my colleagues at California State University, Sacramento, for your kind support and encouragement.

Finally, thank you to my husband, Scott, for his unwavering support in everything I do.

Introduction

THIS COLLECTION OF CASE STUDIES of white-collar crime aims to bridge the gap between textbooks that delve into the theories of white-collar crime and the practice of detecting, investigating, prosecuting, defending, and resolving the crimes in this unique category. Each chapter centers on a criminal case that illustrates one type of white-collar crime often studied in a university-level course on the subject. Using a consistent analytical framework, the case studies examine cases of money laundering, bank fraud, mortgage fraud, affinity fraud, computer crimes, Ponzi schemes, securities fraud, embezzlement, and mail or wire fraud.

Readers will likely not recognize the names in these cases. They were not chosen because of their notoriety—there are plenty of textbooks that discuss Bernie Madoff and Martha Stewart. Rather, these cases were selected because they are, for the most part, run-of-the-mill, typical cases of white-collar crime that investigators, regulators, and prosecutors are likely to encounter. The exceptions to this rule, such as the chapter on mortgage fraud, allow a discussion of additional consequences or legal issues that arose in the course of the investigation or prosecution.

The agencies that investigate and prosecute white-collar crimes tend to cover an array of crimes that is broader than those that occur within a single occupation, and often include financial crimes and political corruption. This book is thus entitled *White-Collar and Financial Crimes* to encompass that broader view. The examples in this supplemental textbook include cases that fit firmly within all definitions of white-collar crime, such as embezzlement and environmental crimes, but also cover money laundering and mortgage fraud, which may not fit within all descriptions.

Many textbooks on the subject of white-collar crime do an excellent job of discussing the various theories at play in these criminal acts. This text is intended not as a substitute for those examinations of theory but as a supplement to them. This book illustrates the theories with real-life examples. In this way, I hope to give students a practical education in what happens during a white-collar crime investigation and prosecution—but also look at what happens before and after.

The case studies of crimes in this book examine fraud using a consistent, four-part framework: crime, investigation, court proceedings, resolution.

THE CRIME

What happened and who did it? This section focuses on how the criminal act began, what the perpetrator's motivation was, the method by which the crime happened, and who the victims were. As much as possible, the focus is on methods and motivations—two factors that investigators and prosecutors seek to understand in similar cases, as do business owners who face the risk of this type of fraud. In the case of embezzlement, for example, the question is what led a bookkeeper to start transferring money out of her employer's account and into her own.

THE INVESTIGATION

How was the crime detected, and how did investigators build a case? Here, the case studies examine how law enforcement got involved and the steps investigators took to document the crime. This section of the chapter typically involves a discussion of which agency was charged with investigating the crime, which in a complex white-collar case can be a complicated jurisdictional issue.

THE COURT PROCEEDINGS

What charges were filed, and how was the case prosecuted? This section discusses the prosecutor's choice of statute and how the facts alleged fit the elements of those criminal laws. In white-collar cases, prosecutors have great discretion in how they charge crimes, including whether to file criminal or civil violations, or to opt for a deferred-prosecution agreement or a nonprosecution agreement. Jurisdictional issues must be decided at this stage, as well, such as whether it is better to bring the case in state or federal court.

Because court proceedings are part of the public record, the prosecutor's court strategy forms a large part of this section of the case study. Those records can also shed light on the defense to the criminal charges, particularly if there was a trial. Even if the case was settled with a guilty plea, court filings can provide insight into the defense strategy.

THE RESOLUTION

Once a defendant is found guilty or negotiates a plea agreement, there is still the question of what the court should do with the defendant. The purposes of sentencing in white-collar cases are similar to those in other criminal convictions. Even if the defendant is a corporation, the sentence is still weighed as to how it fits with the purposes of retribution, rehabilitation, deterrence, incapacitation, and restoration.

In this portion of the chapter, the case study examines how the case was resolved. Was an individual held criminally liable and sentenced to prison? If the defendant was a corporation, how did the court fashion an appropriate sentence? This section focuses on how the sentencing laws applied to the situation, which also illustrates how various factors impact punishment. For example, federal sentencing guidelines for fraud convictions are largely based on the amount of money victims lost, but can also consider the number of victims, whether those victims were members of vulnerable populations, and what role the defendant played in the scheme.

Beyond a prison term or probation, a white-collar case may end in other resolutions, such as fines, restitution, or forfeiture. This offers an opportunity to examine how the victims fared following the resolution of the criminal case. Did they recover any money? Did the victim have to declare bankruptcy? The chapter also looks at broader implications of each case, such as whether laws were changed as a result of the crime, or whether the manner of investigation into such crimes changed.

Every attempt has been made to quantify the damages to the victims, including but not limited to the financial losses. In many cases, victims of white-collar crime lose more than dollars. They lose friends, family members, trust in their churches and social circles, and can even spend years battling the government over tax liabilities that result from the crime.

I have also been mindful that in some of these cases the defendants have served their time and moved on with their lives. As a former criminal defense attorney, I believe that everyone deserves a second chance when they make mistakes and that by spotlighting the cases in this book I could well be bringing those defendants unwanted attention. The source materials for this book are largely public documents and news accounts that are widely available. To minimize further stigma to the defendants who are out of prison, I have used their first names and initials in the text. All cases, however, are cited in full with the defendants' names in the notes at the end of each chapter.

ONE

Embezzlement

UNITED STATES V. TAMMIE C.

EMBEZZLEMENT IS ONE OF THE MOST COMMON white-collar crimes. The FBI defines embezzlement as the "unlawful misappropriation or misapplication by an offender to his/her own use or purpose of money, property, or some other thing of value entrusted to his/her care, custody, or control" (FBI, 2001). In other words, embezzlement occurs when employees steal money or property from employers.

Businesses are plagued by employee theft—whether they know it or not, and whether they admit it or not. A precise estimate of loss due to embezzlement is difficult to calculate. Embezzlement is not a separate category in most official databases, which means that these cases are included in the larger category of larceny. Further complicating a financial tally is the fact that some businesses are reluctant to report the crime. Business owners often choose to handle the theft in-house out of fear that publicly acknowledging weak controls would reflect poorly on the business (NWCCC, 2016).

Despite these challenges, a 2013 study by the Association of Certified Fraud Examiners (ACFE) estimated global losses from embezzlement at $3.7 trillion (ACFE, 2014). This makes employee theft two to three times more costly than all other Part I index crimes combined, which includes murder, robbery, assault, burglary, and other serious and violent offenses. And that doesn't include the collateral costs to employers who are victims, including legal and accounting expenses, time away from the business to deal with an investigation, higher insurance premiums, and the lost opportunities to invest profits in expanding a company.

In his seminal work on fraud, Donald Cressey theorized that there were three factors commonly seen in these cases, forming what he called the Fraud Triangle (Cressey, 1953). "Trusted persons become trust violators," Cressey observed, "when they conceive of themselves as having a financial problem which is non-shareable, are aware this problem can be secretly resolved by violation of the position of financial trust, and are able to apply to their own conduct in that situation verbalizations which enable them to adjust their conceptions of themselves as trusted persons with their conceptions of themselves as users of the entrusted funds or property" (p. 30).

Pressure is what first motivates the crime. The individual has some financial problem that they are unable to solve through legitimate means, so they begin to consider committing an illegal act. The person must also have an *opportunity* to abuse a position of trust in order to solve this financial problem with low perceived risk of getting caught. And, as most offenders in these crimes are first-time offenders, they must be able to *rationalize* their conduct in a way that makes it acceptable or justifiable. For example, an employee might justify theft by telling herself that she is only "borrowing" the money and will repay it later, or that she deserves the money because she is underpaid by her employer.

A global study of occupational fraud and abuse by the Association of Certified Fraud Examiners noted that smaller organizations tended to suffer disproportionately larger losses, which may be a function of small businesses having fewer prevention programs in place (ACFE, 2014). As an example, organizations with tip lines and other antifraud controls saw reduced losses to fraud and tended to catch the financial misuse earlier.

Of the three classifications of occupational fraud that ACFE looked at—asset misappropriation, corruption, and financial statement fraud—the theft of assets was the most common, occurring in 85 percent of the cases studied. The median loss in that category was $130,000. More than three-quarters of frauds studied were committed by workers in accounting, operations, sales, executive or upper management, customer service, purchasing, and finance. And most of the offenders had no criminal record that would have tipped off an employer; only 5 percent had prior convictions for fraud. More than 80 percent of offenders had not been previously punished or terminated by an employer for fraud-related conduct.

As you read the following case, consider how the embezzlement at Obermiller Construction Services mirrors the findings of these studies. Note, too, how Cressey's Fraud Triangle might apply in this case. This case also illustrates the many collateral harms caused when a trusted employee commits embezzlement against a small business.

In 2000, Obermiller Construction Services experienced the kind of good fortune that nearly all small business owners hope for. After several years of middling returns, the Missouri-based commercial paving company landed a big client. In fact, the biggest: Walmart.

The contract came about after owner Cheryl Obermiller hit a pothole in a Walmart parking lot and blew out a tire. When she called to complain, she also mentioned that her company, located a short drive away, could have prevented that problem. Within weeks, the corporation agreed, hiring Cheryl's company to patch the pavement for that store and others in the region. Suddenly, the family-run business needed to buy new trucks, hire crews, and expand in ways that Cheryl couldn't have imagined (Obermiller, 2019).

Cheryl's savior arrived in the form of Tammie C., a bookkeeper who came with excellent references and a track record of helping businesses just like Obermiller Construction. She was easy to get along with and had a sharp mind. Best of all, she had good, enthusiastic references from trusted professionals. Cheryl welcomed Tammie aboard in August 2001, and soon the bookkeeper was handling all of the company's finances, including reconciling the bank accounts, paying taxes and insurance, and maintaining the accounts receivable and payable. Tammie proved to be an excellent employee—reliable and with a great recall of facts and figures. Bills were promptly paid and Tammie always provided thorough reports on the company's accounts. Obermiller Construction grew by huge leaps over the next few years. Cheryl was busier than ever, but she had faith that Tammie was handling the finances because there had been no problems.

One wintry day in January 2010, a snowstorm kept Tammie from coming into the office, and Cheryl got the mail, which was usually Tammie's job. Among the mail, Cheryl found a certified letter from the IRS about past-due tax payments. The tone was alarming. The IRS threatened to seize the company's bank accounts because Obermiller Construction had ignored the agency's letters for six months. Cheryl called Tammie, but her trusted bookkeeper assured her that it was a misunderstanding and she had been working to resolve it. Tammie promised to take care of it when she came to work the next day.

But Cheryl wasn't willing to wait. She called the IRS and learned that the company hadn't paid payroll taxes for the first quarter of 2009. In the second quarter of 2009, the company had filed a return, but had not submitted the payment. But in the third quarter, filings and payments had returned to normal. Cheryl was convinced this was a glitch and her money had been credited to the wrong account. The IRS put the case on hold for a month so Cheryl could provide documents to prove it was a mistake.

When she called Tammie back to give her the update, her accountant's demeanor was changed. Tammie's once-precise recall of facts and figures gave way to vague, stumbling responses to even basic questions. The call made Cheryl uncomfortable and she knew something was wrong.

"I got off the phone and went through her computer," she said (C. Obermiller, personal communication, September 4, 2018). "I looked through Tammie's desk drawer and found blank checks, some that she had signed. Then I found the tax notices and I knew that she was lying. She knew the taxes weren't paid."

In the back of Tammie's desk drawer, Cheryl found a folder containing six months of IRS letters demanding payment. The letters were neatly organized with the envelopes stapled to them and dated in Tammie's handwriting. The government wanted the money—a lot of it—that Obermiller Construction hadn't paid.

Cheryl's immediate instinct was to lock down anything financial until she had more information. She called her bank and instructed it not to put through any checks unless it cleared them with her. Before she left for the day, Cheryl told her sons, who worked at Obermiller Construction's office, "If Tammie comes in early, don't let her go back to her office."

While Cheryl was on her way to the office the next morning, the bank called to say that two checks had come in overnight. One was a normal utility payment. The other was a check to Tammie for $3,760, signed by Cheryl—only Cheryl had not signed the check. The signature had been forged. The bank pulled every check from Obermiller accounts from the previous few months for Cheryl to review and ordered copies of archived checks to compare signatures. That afternoon, the bank manager came to Cheryl's office, and the two identified $27,000 in forged checks—and that was only from the past few months.

"I was in such complete shell shock. It was unbelievable," Cheryl said.

That was when she called the police.

THE INVESTIGATION

Initially, Cheryl worked with her bank and a local police detective to uncover the full extent of the fraud. Eventually, the police and local district attorney referred the criminal investigation to the Federal Bureau of Investigation. The FBI agent asked a lot of routine questions about Tammie and her role in the office. Did she get the mail? Did she answer the phones? Did she have access to checks? Did she pay the bills? Did she balance the checkbook? (Obermiller, 2019). The answer was yes to all of these questions.

The investigation uncovered both simple and complicated methods of fraud perpetrated by Cheryl's accountant. With the help of a forensic accountant and her bank manager, Cheryl went over a decade's worth of checks, debit card expenditures, and account statements. The first forged check was from December 2001, about four months after Tammie was hired. From that point, it appeared, Tammie had gradually become more confident that no one would uncover the misuse of company funds.

Tammie used a debit card that had been assigned to a former employee. Rather than closing it when the employee left the company, Tammie made internal transfers to fund the account and used the money for herself. The company had paid for airline tickets, amusement parks entry fees, and hotel rooms for vacations. Cheryl's business had filled the fuel tanks of Tammie's family cars twice a week for years, and had paid for Tammie's craft supplies, donations to a local school, and many meals. Most infuriating, one year, Tammie had charged expensive Christmas gifts for Cheryl and her husband— gifts that Cheryl had insisted were too extravagant (Obermiller, 2019).

Tammie also wrote checks to herself and signed Cheryl's name, cashing the checks at her own bank, across the state line in Kansas (Plea Agreement, 2011). In addition, Tammie had manipulated the payroll system so that she didn't pay her share of the health insurance premiums for herself and her family.

The most serious financial impropriety was the failure to pay the two quarters of payroll taxes in 2009. At the time, Obermiller Construction had had the money to pay the IRS. Cheryl recalled that she had met with Tammie about the company's financial status to determine if it could buy a new, $55,000 truck. Tammie had assured her that the company did have the cash on hand to invest in the new equipment, so the purchase went forward. That money should have gone toward the tax payment before making any new investment in the company's expansion.

Not long after the missed payment, the IRS began sending letters. But because Tammie retrieved and opened all the mail, no one else saw the increasingly urgent warnings that the company was in arrears with the US government. The financial sleight of hand was also kept hidden in detailed reports that Tammie prepared for Cheryl that showed where every dollar went. Cheryl wouldn't know for years that those reports were fiction. It didn't occur to her that she hadn't seen the source documents for any of the figures.

Between the unpaid taxes and subsequent interest and penalties, the forged checks, and the diverted funds, Cheryl estimated that she lost over $1 million through the embezzlement. And there were other indirect costs. The business had turned down work that would've required an investment of capital that it did not have. That could have resulted in profits and additional growth, though it is difficult to quantify that type of loss. After the embezzlement, Obermiller Construction kept personnel to a minimum and cut expenses to the bone in order to survive. Cheryl and her husband had personally guaranteed the company's debt and had the most at risk. But employees and their families were also affected by the company's finances. Instead of keeping people working on maintenance tasks during the off-season, Cheryl had to let people go. Previously scheduled raises had to be delayed. The company also made fewer purchases and had to negotiate with suppliers to pay their bills late.

There was an emotional cost to embezzlement as well. The day Cheryl discovered the IRS notice, she went home in a state of shock. "The rest of that day, and many others after, I operated in kind of a fog. I was so stunned that I could barely breathe. I remember listening to the banker and the detective discussing what they saw, what else to look for and how to proceed, but I just sat there in a complete daze" (Obermiller, 2019, p. 28). It was unfathomable that Tammie was stealing. She was the most trusted employee in the company.

THE PROSECUTION

Federal law enforcement doesn't always get involved with embezzlement cases, but in the Obermiller Construction case, the loss amount was high and the US government had jurisdiction because of the interstate transfer of the stolen money. As part of the scheme to defraud her employer, Tammie forged checks from Obermiller Construction drawn on a bank in Missouri, and deposited them in her bank, located in Kansas (18 U.S.C. § 1344, Bank Fraud; see sidebar 1.1).

In 2011, Tammie C. was named in a single-count information that charged her with bank fraud, a violation of 18 U.S.C. § 1344 (Information, 2011). The

STATUTE

18 U.S.C. § 1344

Bank Fraud

Whoever knowingly executes, or attempts to execute, a scheme or artifice—

(1) to defraud a financial institution; or

(2) to obtain any of the moneys, funds, credits, assets, securities, or other property owned by, or under the custody or control of, a financial institution, by means of false or fraudulent pretenses, representations, or promises; shall be fined not more than $1,000,000 or imprisoned not more than 30 years, or both.

information incorporated a variety of fraudulent acts between 2004 and 2009, with losses to Obermiller Construction amounting to $437,942. The case was filed in the United States District Court for the Western District of Missouri.

The prosecutors alleged a fraud scheme that included $213,590 in forged checks and more than $40,000 lost to the misuse of company debit card accounts. The information also accused Tammie of failing to deduct about $60,000 in health and dental insurance premiums from payroll checks for her family members and other employees. She was also charged with failure to pay $176,000 in Kansas state sales tax, which resulted in additional interest and penalties of $85,000. And the government alleged that Tammie had failed to make federal tax payments of $23,532 in 2009, resulting in penalties of $37,422.

A violation of 18 U.S.C. § 1344 is a Class B felony and carries a sentencing range from probation to 30 years in prison, a fine up to $1 million, and as many as 5 years of supervised release. The actual sentence is determined by a complex calculation under the United States Sentencing Guidelines that considers many factors, including the defendant's criminal history and the loss amount related to the crime.

On the same day that the information was filed, Tammie pleaded guilty in a negotiated plea agreement in which she admitted to all the charges alleged.

In fraud cases, sentencing is based in large part on § 2B1.1 of the United States Sentencing Guidelines (USSG). The Guidelines were enacted in 1987 and were mandatory until 2005, when the Supreme Court, in *United States v. Booker* (543 U.S. 220 [2005]), held that the Guidelines were only advisory. The Sentencing Guidelines are still the starting point for calculating a sentence.

For convictions involving fraud, the Guidelines consider numerous factors that weigh in determining a defendant's culpability—such as the loss amount, the person's role in the offense, the number of victims, and the defendant's criminal history. The most important factor is the loss amount. In Tammie's plea agreement, the government and defendant agreed to a loss amount of approximately $473,942, going back to 2004. That didn't cover the entire period that Cheryl believed Tammie had been embezzling funds, but the statute of limitations might make proving all of the losses impossible.

In her guilty plea, Tammie admitted to a single count of bank fraud, the factual basis for which was a June 2009 check for $4,050, payable to Tammie and deposited in her bank in Kansas. The check was drawn on the Obermiller Construction payroll account, which was held at a bank in Missouri. Tammie had forged the signature on the check. These facts met the legal requirements for a conviction under 18 U.S.C. § 1344.

In addition to that charged offense, Tammie admitted to other related criminal conduct. This included forged checks in the amount of $213,000, misuse of debit cards totaling more than $40,000, and failure to pay insurance premiums from payroll checks for her own family and other employees, which cost the company nearly $60,000. Tammie also admitted failing to pay sales tax to the state of Kansas in the amount of $176,000, which cost the company $84,500 in penalties. Further, she admitted failing to pay the required federal tax deposits of $23,500, which resulted in penalties of more than $37,000. In total, the loss amount from 2004 to 2009 was nearly a half million dollars.

The plea agreement made clear that Tammie was responsible for the $4,050 from the charged conduct, and also for *relevant conduct*. Relevant conduct is defined as uncharged related criminal activity and can be considered by the court in fashioning a sentence (USSG § 1B1.3(a)(3)). Relevant conduct can be uncharged conduct or, in cases that go to trial, can even encompass acquitted conduct. The conduct must be proven by a preponderance of the evidence in the sentencing proceedings, but does not have to meet the higher burden of proof beyond a reasonable doubt, as it would at trial.

A plea agreement is a contract between the prosecutor and the defendant that sets out the boundaries of what each party will argue at the sentencing hearing. In Tammie's case, the parties agreed to certain Sentencing Guidelines under USSG § 2B1.1. This Guideline addresses financial crimes such as mail fraud, wire fraud, and bank fraud. The federal Sentencing Guidelines attempt to quantify loss into a points system. In this case, a fraud conviction has a base offense level of 7. The loss amount under § 2B1.1(b)(1)(H), between $400,000 and $1 million, added twelve levels, for a total offense level of 19.

A defendant who pleads guilty is entitled to up to three levels off for acceptance of responsibility (USSG § 3E1.1(b)). In Tammie C.'s case, the United States agreed not to seek an upward departure from the guidelines, and the defendant agreed not to seek a downward departure from the guidelines. In general, the agreement between the parties is not binding on the judge nor on the probation office, which completes a presentence investigation and advises the judge as to sentencing.

The agreement also called for Tammie to pay restitution to Obermiller Construction in the amount of $472,000.

THE RESOLUTION

Cheryl estimated that her business lost far more than the amount the defendant and the government agreed upon. She'd found evidence of theft dating back to December 2001, but those transactions were beyond the five-year statute of limitations. In addition, Tammie's sentence was based on a loss amount between $400,000 and $1 million. To have lengthened Tammie's sentence, the government would have had to show that she caused a loss of more than $1 million, and Cheryl didn't believe she could prove that much in direct loss.

Those other, indirect losses included interest on the missing capital and lost opportunities to expand the business, take on large projects, or hire new workers—growth that the company might have been able to undertake if Obermiller Construction had not been the victim of embezzlement. Cheryl also estimated that she spent tens of thousands of dollars on forensic accountants and lawyers to get a true accounting of the loss and an accurate picture of her company's finances. And all of that effort took time, as well. It would take her years to resolve the financial mess and get the company back on stable ground.

She also lost a friend who was practically a family member. This was a small business, and Cheryl and Tammie had worked side by side for years. Their families had been close.

At the sentencing hearing, Cheryl made a victim impact statement, asking the court to impose a sentence commensurate with the time that Tammie was stealing from the company, plus how long Cheryl estimated it would take for her to recover her loss. She asked for a sentence of fifteen years. That was half of the maximum sentence permitted by law and was in Cheryl's mind a more proportional punishment.

The court disagreed and followed the sentencing recommendation of the parties—a sentence of thirty-three months in prison, restitution of the loss amount, and five years of supervision following her release from incarceration.

Once Tammie pleaded guilty, Obermiller Construction issued a 1099 to her for nearly $500,000—the amount she had admitted to stealing—for previously undeclared income.

THE AFTERMATH

It took several months for Cheryl to get a full picture of the harm to her business. Her immediate concern was how to pay the overdue taxes and keep her business operating. She eventually negotiated a settlement with the governments involved to pay the sales taxes to the state of Kansas and the 2009 quarterly tax payments to the IRS.

But those negotiations were hard-fought and painful. The government agencies did not care that Cheryl was the victim of a crime—Obermiller Construction owed back taxes and needed to pay. Threats to seize the company continued as Cheryl struggled to pay the taxes and interest on the late payments.

"I am unaware of any other crime that allows government officials to so effectively and aggressively persecute and punish the victims. As part of setting up a payment agreement with the IRS, I had to fill out forms that required me to give an itemized list of every asset I owned. I do not know if I can adequately express how it felt to be on the brink of bankruptcy as the result of a crime, and then have to give a list providing the value of my living room furniture and wedding rings to the IRS, as security against the resulting tax debt" (Obermiller, 2019, p. 284).

It was only once Cheryl sought help from her congressional representative that her IRS problems improved, with the tax agency agreeing to waive penalties on the tax debt and set up a payment plan that let her stay in business. Prior to that, the IRS wanted her to liquidate all her equipment and assets to repay the overdue bill, which would have closed the doors on Obermiller Construction Services. It still took years to repay the IRS. Bankruptcy might have been easier, Cheryl said, but she wanted to keep her business alive. "If my bank and business vendors would work with me, then I could make it work and pay everyone back."

The company survived only because Cheryl's creditors and vendors were sympathetic and didn't force her into bankruptcy. Those small businesses suffered, too, because she had to pay her bills late in order to prioritize payments on the back taxes. But they worked with her because they understood her predicament. Every time she explained what happened and asked for more time to pay, her vendors admitted that they also had been victims of employee theft or knew someone who had.

"I paid back every dime to every vendor," Cheryl said. "I offered to pay in full if they would waive late fees. Some did, some reduced them, but not a single person took me to court. By doing that, they gave up their right to sue me and file liens. But so many people in the business had been victims themselves."

To date, Obermiller Construction has not been repaid. Though Tammie was ordered to pay restitution, under the terms of her plea agreement she could not take any job with fiduciary responsibility while she was under supervision. This limited her income and, thus, the 10 percent of pretax earnings that was garnished from her wages.

As she put her business back together, Cheryl was determined to make it stronger and impervious to theft in the future. She studied embezzlement and learned that her case is entirely too typical. Eventually, Cheryl put everything she learned firsthand and through her studies into a book for small-business owners. Using her experience, she now advises others how to avoid embezzlement.

Her top three tips for business owners are:

1. Get your own mail and go through it.
2. Lock up checks and credit cards.
3. Check bank statements online every day.

REFERENCES

ACFE (Association of Certified Fraud Examiners). (2014). *Report to the Nations on Occupational Fraud and Abuse*. http://www.acfe.com/rttn/docs/2014-report-to-nations.pdf.

Cressey, D. (1953). *Other People's Money*. Glencoe, IL: Free Press.

FBI (Federal Bureau of Investigation). (2001). *Crime in the United States, 2000*. Washington, DC. https://ucr.fbi.gov/crime-in-the-u.s/2010/crime-in-the-u.s.-2010/offense-definitions.

Information. (2011). United States v. Cowell, 4:11-cr-00056-GAF, W. Dist. Missouri. March 8.

NWCCC (National White Collar Crime Center). (2016). "Embezzlemen t/Employee Theft." *NW3C*. Accessed January 10, 2018. http://www.nw3c.org /docs/research/embezzlement-employee-theft.pdf.

Obermiller, C. (2019). *Fraud Point: The Small Business Owner's Guide to Outwitting Embezzlers, Thieves, and Scallywags*. United Kingdom: PotHole Press.

Plea Agreement (2011.) United States v. Cowell, 4:11-cr-00057-GAF. W. Dist. Missouri. March 8.

Mortgage Fraud

UNITED STATES V. RONNIE DUKE

UNLIKE MANY OF THE OTHER CASES in this book, the mortgage fraud scheme detailed in this chapter is not a typical case. It was the largest mortgage fraud case in Michigan history. The investigation involved 500 mortgages on more than 180 properties, with more than 100 straw buyers. Lenders lost approximately $100 million.

But in many respects, it's the perfect case study for learning about this category of white-collar crime, because the vast enterprise discussed in this chapter used a variety of tactics to defraud lenders, including fake documents, straw buyers, and corruption among players in the industry. The scheme also broke new ground in fraud, including the use of an entirely bogus escrow company that facilitated "ghost" loans—mortgages on houses that were never sold, leaving the lenders wholly unsecured. The story of *United States v. Ronnie Duke* also contains several twists that are not solely related to white-collar crime but that can arise in any criminal case and, therefore, are valuable to study, particularly for the insight they offer into the motivation behind the conduct.

Before learning about how this mortgage fraud case operated, it's important to understand the basics of the housing market and the lending process and how regulations were supposed to stop this sort of criminal activity.

OVERVIEW OF LENDING PRACTICES

In late 2008, the United States economy suffered a devastating collapse. While multiple segments of the financial industry contributed to the Great Recession, one of the causes was undoubtedly the high-risk lending strategy of mortgage companies and banks that were cashing in on the superhot housing market. Starting in 2003, the mortgage industry expanded into subprime loans (Financial Crisis Inquiry Commission, 2011). These were financial instruments that had originally been strictly for borrowers who had bad credit or lacked funds of their own to invest in a house. The interest rates were high—sometimes double what a buyer with good credit could get with a conventional loan.

Subprime lending thrived as the housing market grew, and lenders kept coming up with ever more creative financing options, like no- or low-verification loans, negative-amortization mortgages, and NINJA loans (no income, no job or assets) (PSI Report, 2011). When the tide of easy money and low-interest teaser rate loans went out, it became apparent that large parts of the mortgage industry had been rife with fraud. As the housing bubble burst, home prices plummeted, leaving owners with debt that far exceeded any equity in their property. What followed was a foreclosure wave that affected millions of families.

To address the fallout, President Barack Obama created the Financial Fraud Enforcement Task Force, a collaboration among federal agencies, along with state, local, and tribal law enforcement partners, to address mortgage fraud and other financial crimes (Financial Crisis Inquiry Commission, 2011). The Mortgage Fraud Working Group, a component of that effort, was based in Sacramento, and was led by Ben Wagner, US attorney for the Eastern District of California. Congress allotted millions of dollars to the Department of Justice to investigate the causes of the financial crash. The first wave of mortgage fraud prosecutions started not long thereafter. Although prosecuted across the country, the mortgage fraud cases were largely concentrated in states and districts where the housing market collapse was felt most acutely, such as California and Florida.

Mortgage fraud comes in many different flavors. A home buyer signs the loan application under a notice that providing false information violates the law, so inflating income or lying about the source of a down payment can be a criminal act. It is also illegal for property to be purchased by a straw buyer who has no intent to live in the house and whose personal information and good credit score are used to qualify for a mortgage. In such cases, a person who would not qualify for a mortgage pays the straw buyer a flat fee and takes control of the property once the purchase is complete. Also clearly against the law is fabricating fraudulent income and tax documents to trick the lender into approving a mortgage.

There is no actual "mortgage fraud" statute in the *United States Code*. There is a bank fraud statute, 18 U.S.C. § 1344, which applies to lending institutions that are federally insured under the Federal Deposit Insurance Corporation (FDIC). But the bank fraud statute doesn't apply to loans made through lenders that aren't banks, such as Countrywide, Washington Mutual, and Novastar—all major players in the housing market in the early to mid-2000s. Rather, prosecutors often rely on other statutes to charge those accused of fraud in the housing market, including wire fraud (18 U.S.C. § 1343), mail fraud (18 U.S.C. § 1341), and conspiracy (18 U.S.C. § 1349).

Despite the lack of a specific statute, the crime of mortgage fraud does get its own entry in the United States attorneys' annual report. In 2012, federal prosecutors filed 423 new mortgage fraud cases, and reported 837 guilty verdicts or pleas, and 4 not-guilty verdicts (Annual Statistical Report, 2012). Since then, those numbers have steadily dropped. In 2017, the US Attorneys' Annual Statistical Report recorded 44 new cases of mortgage fraud, 158 guilty pleas or verdicts, and 2 not-guilty verdicts (Annual Statistical Report, 2017).

To fully appreciate the breadth and depth of the fraudulent activity in the following case study, it's important to know how the lending process typically works. A home buyer usually gets prequalified for a mortgage, with the lender setting a maximum amount to be loaned based on the applicant's income, assets, and outstanding debt. From those figures, a debt-to-income ratio is derived. The proposed loan amount is added to all existing debt to determine the buyer's ability to service the new payments.

Interest rates are determined by this matrix as well, with low-risk borrowers getting the more favorable rates. High-risk borrowers, such as those with a poor credit score or low income, may be charged a higher interest rate because they're considered more at risk of defaulting. The lender also looks at whether the borrower is going to live in the house or use it as an investment property. Typically, the bank considers buyers who are going to use the property as their primary residence a better credit risk as they have a greater incentive to make the monthly payments.

Once the borrower makes an offer on a house, the lender verifies the information necessary to secure the loan—income, credit history, and the value of other assets. A mortgage is secured by the property, so if a borrower does not pay, the lender can take possession of the property. So the lender also requires an inspection of the property and an appraisal in order to ensure that the value of the property matches or exceeds the amount of the loan. In a title search, the previous ownership records are examined for any outstanding liens on the property that might interfere with the lender's ability to secure its interest. Lenders want to be in the first position, or the first in line to repossess the property if the borrower defaults on the mortgage. Any outstanding liens must be paid when the property is transferred to a new owner.

All of the information is entered into a HUD-1 form, a master index of debts, liens to be paid, verified income and assets, and the property's value. Once this information is complete and verified, the buyer finishes the purchase at a closing, a procedure, generally held at a title company, during which the buyer signs all the necessary paperwork to transfer title of the property. The title company files the transfer of the deed with county officials and thus secures the mortgage by placing a lien on that property.

THE CASE

Besides the largest mortgage fraud case in Michigan history, it was also one of the largest in US history. The investigation encompassed more than five hundred fraudulent mortgages and dozens of individuals who were involved—either as participants, witnesses, or victims. The scheme, which ran from the fall of 2003 through approximately July 2007 in Wayne County, Michigan, embraced the more traditional mortgage fraud schemes, where loan applicants submitted materially false information. It also included "ghost" loans that involved fraudulent title companies, unknowing owners of properties that were leveraged, and other fictitious aspects of the fraud. Of the hundreds of mortgages investigated by the FBI in this case, more than 80 percent went into default and were foreclosed on. Lenders reported losses of $100 million.

At the top of the scheme was Ronnie Duke. Though he dropped out of high school in ninth grade, Duke seemed to have made a success of himself as the owner of Hardcore Racing, a prominent name in the world of drag racing. He also owned First Escrow Company, LLC, and styled himself as a real estate investor. But the escrow company was simply a front for a larger, wholly fraudulent enterprise—a mortgage fraud empire that was instrumental in amassing 180 properties purchased with fraudulent mortgages (Complaint, 2010).

The home loans that Duke and his colleagues secured illustrate various types of mortgage fraud. Some of the fraudulent transactions were loans taken out by straw buyers—nominal purchasers who are used for their good credit but who will not have control of the property. Applicants' incomes were inflated to induce banks to lend money, and borrowers would frequently lie about the source of their down payment. Lease agreements were submitted to the lender to prove the property would provide a stream of rental income in the future. In some instances, borrowers would claim that they intended to use the house as their primary residence, when that was not their intent. Finally, Duke and his associates would transfer large sums of money to the borrower's bank account to show the lender that the buyer had significant funds available—though the funds were removed once the verification of deposit was completed. These misrepresentations are typical in mortgage fraud schemes.

There was a second category of mortgages as well. The players in the scheme called these transactions "ghost" loans. *Nothing* about them was real. The "seller" either was unaware of the sale of the property or might be a straw buyer from one of the other "real" mortgage transactions (Complaint, 2010). The purchase agreement between the borrower and the seller was fake. The borrower would apply for a loan to purchase the property, stating that his intention was to rent it as an investment property. A fake lease agreement would justify the future rental income. Or the borrower would falsely claim that they intended to live in the house. The borrower's bank account would again be infused to show a large balance, but only until the bank had completed the verification of deposit.

In some respects, the ghost loans were similar to the real mortgage transactions. The same misleading documents were submitted to lenders—fake lease agreements, false statements that this house would be the borrower's primary residence, inflated bank balances to pass the lender's deposit verification. But there were key differences. In the ghost loans, the person listed as the seller might be unaware that their property was being sold. Or the purported seller might be one of Duke's employees or a prior "customer" from one of the straw purchaser mortgages. Because there was no actual sale intended, the sales agreement to purchase the property was also bogus.

Other features also made the ghost loans fraudulent. Cashier's checks, which purported to represent 20 percent of the purchase price as a down payment, were canceled and never deposited. The title insurance documents showing that the seller had clear title to the property and that the mortgage lender's lien on the property would be in first position were counterfeit. And the warranty deed purporting to transfer title from the seller to the borrower was fabricated to deceive the lender and was never recorded in the county register of deeds. Similarly, the mortgage document that purported to secure the borrower's debt was falsified and was never recorded with the county. As there was no real closing or settlement of the loan, the HUD-1 settlement statement was also drafted only to deceive the lender.

The paperwork looked convincing, and lenders transferred funds to the "sellers" to complete the purchase. The money allowed the players to continue the scheme by making monthly payments on real and ghost loans, and making down payments to legitimate sellers of residential properties purchased with the real loans. Sometimes the same residential property would be used simultaneously as collateral for a real loan and for two or more ghost loans, with all of the mortgages funded by different lenders.

When a buyer makes a down payment of less than 20 percent of the purchase price, lenders require escrow accounts, where money is held pending the verification of the mortgage information. For this reason, Duke and his coschemers applied for loans that required a 20 percent down payment. Also, by structuring the scheme this way, the lenders wouldn't be responsible for paying the real estate taxes on the properties. Instead, Duke would pay the taxes, thus ensuring that the taxing authority didn't get payments from multiple lenders on the same property—which might tip off authorities to the scheme. At the end of a ghost loan transaction, when the lenders transferred the funds to pay the "seller" for the property, instead of having a lien in first position, they were completely unsecured. If the buyer defaulted on the loan, the lender would not be able to foreclose on the property to recover what it was owed.

Duke's scheme required partners who played various roles: straw buyers, recruiters of new straw purchasers, loan processors, mortgage brokers, and someone who controlled the flow of money (Complaint, 2010). Managing the complex scheme was vital to keep it from being detected. Duke and his coschemers had to keep up with monthly mortgage payments so lenders wouldn't foreclose, which might alert authorities to the fraud. At one point, Duke was paying $1.3 million a month in mortgage payments. The money to cover that tab came from new loans, creating more debt that had to be serviced.

There were other expenses, too. Straw buyers earned between $5,000 and $15,000 per transaction, and others earned commissions on each sale. The rest of the money was paid to other participants and to finance the scheme and unrelated businesses—including motorsports companies and a night-club. The players spent money freely, buying themselves expensive cars, boats, real property, and trips overseas. Duke bought himself a helicopter.

THE INVESTIGATION

In June 2006, the Federal Bureau of Investigation began looking into Duke's business. But before agents made their investigation known, Duke approached them. In June 2007, he walked into the federal building and told the agents everything—his entire lifestyle was funded through a web of complex mortgage fraud schemes. He began cooperating with the FBI.

Duke started making audio and video recordings under FBI supervision, capturing his coconspirators taking part in the scheme. At one meeting at a Cracker Barrel restaurant, Duke wore a recording device to ensnare five others who were later charged in the scheme (Transcript, Sentencing Hearing, 2013, p. 49). He helped the special agents identify properties involved in the conspiracy and walked them through how it worked. This was no easy task. The investigation had identified hundreds of suspect mortgages and proper-ties. Duke explained the structure of the organization and gave details on hundreds of loan files that he voluntarily turned over, even categorizing them as real or ghost loans.

His information helped the FBI establish probable cause for seven search warrants, and he consented to the FBI's search of his home and business. In all, more than one hundred boxes of evidence were seized. Duke forfeited $1.4 million in assets that had been paid for by the fraud. And in preparation for the end of the investigation, he downsized his company—going from fifty employees to fifteen and moving his racing operation to a smaller space.

Duke testified before the grand jury and was prepared to testify at the trials of those whom he had worked with over the course of the four-year scheme. It is not typical for prosecutors to turn the organizer of a scheme into a cooperator. More often, the government looks for lower-level individu-als who will cooperate against the more culpable players in the scheme. In this case, Duke turned himself in and offered testimony against his coconspirators in this unprecedented mortgage fraud case. Due to his cooperation, fifteen of Duke's coconspirators were charged with fraud.

THE PROSECUTION

The government elected to charge Duke with a single-count indictment, alleging a violation of 18 U.S.C. § 1349, conspiracy to commit wire fraud (see sidebar 2.1). The conspiracy count covered all of the fraudulent mortgage transactions that Duke's operation encompassed.

As Duke was already cooperating with the government, it was not a surprise that he pleaded guilty to the conspiracy charge in July 2012. Before the court can accept a guilty plea, a defendant must admit to the facts that provide a basis for the charge. The factual basis is included in the plea agreement document signed by the defendant and the prosecutor. In Duke's agreement, he admitted to conspiring with five codefendants to defraud mortgage lenders out of millions of dollars and to leading and organizing the scheme (Plea Agreement, 2012). The agreement also detailed the fraud scheme, including how the real and ghost loans worked, what types of fake documents were submitted, and how Duke used the First Escrow business to act as a fake closing company to receive interstate wire transfers from lenders.

Duke recruited others to participate in the fraud, including straw buyers, loan processors, mortgage brokers, and appraisers. He admitted to using the ill-gotten funds for his business, Hardcore Racing, and to purchase expensive cars and a helicopter.

In exchange for his substantial assistance and extensive cooperation in the investigation up to that point, the defendant and the government agreed to recommend that the court impose a sentence of not more than 15 years' imprisonment. In addition, the government agreed to file a separate motion under the United States Sentencing Guidelines (§ 5K1.1), seeking a further reduction of his sentence to reward Duke's continued cooperation between the time of the guilty plea and his sentencing hearing. This statute gives the government the discretion to recommend a lower sentence based on the value of the defendant's assistance and cooperation. In Duke's case, the plea agreement capped the sentence at 15 years. But the government's recommendation could be as little as 10 years if Duke's additional assistance merited a lower sentence.

Duke had what is known as a *binding plea agreement,* pursuant to Federal Rules of Criminal Procedure 11(c)(1)(C) (see sidebar 2.1). Under this rule, the

18 USC § 1349. Attempt and Conspiracy

Any person who attempts or conspires to commit any offense under this chapter shall be subject to the same penalties as those prescribed for the offense, the commission of which was the object of the attempt or conspiracy.

18 U.S.C. § 1343. Wire Fraud

Whoever, having devised or intending to devise any scheme or artifice to defraud, or for obtaining money or property by means of false or fraudulent pretenses, representations, or promises, transmits or causes to be transmitted by means of wire, radio, or television communication in interstate or foreign commerce, any writings, signs, signals, pictures, or sounds for the purpose of executing such scheme or artifice, shall be fined under this title or imprisoned not more than 20 years, or both. If the violation occurs in relation to, or involving any benefit authorized, transported, transmitted, transferred, disbursed, or paid in connection with, a presidentially declared major disaster or emergency (as those terms are defined in section 102 of the Robert T. Stafford Disaster Relief and Emergency Assistance Act (42 U.S.C. § 5122)), or affects a financial institution, such person shall be fined not more than $1,000,000 or imprisoned not more than 30 years, or both.

18 U.S.C. § 111(a)(1) & (b)

(a) In General. Whoever—

(1) forcibly assaults, resists, opposes, impedes, intimidates, or interferes with any person designated in section 1114 of this title while engaged in or on account of the performance of official duties; or

(2) forcibly assaults or intimidates any person who formerly served as a person designated in section 1114 on account of the performance of official duties during such person's term of service,

shall, where the acts in violation of this section constitute only simple assault, be fined under this title or imprisoned not more than one year, or both, and where such acts involve physical contact with the victim of that assault or the intent to commit another felony, be fined under this title or imprisoned not more than 8 years, or both.

(b) Enhanced Penalty.—

Whoever, in the commission of any acts described in subsection (a), uses a deadly or dangerous weapon (including a weapon intended to cause death or danger but that fails to do so by reason of a defective component) or inflicts bodily injury, shall be fined under this title or imprisoned not more than 20 years, or both.

18 U.S.C. § 751

(a) Whoever escapes or attempts to escape from the custody of the Attorney General or his authorized representative, or from any institution or facility in which he is confined by direction of the Attorney General, or from any custody under or by virtue of any process issued under the laws of the United States by any court, judge, or magistrate judge, or from the custody of an officer or employee of the United States pursuant to lawful arrest, shall, if the custody or confinement is by virtue of an arrest on a charge of felony, or conviction of any offense, be fined under this title or imprisoned not more than five years, or both; or if the custody or confinement is for extradition, or for exclusion or expulsion proceedings under the immigration laws, or by virtue of an arrest or charge of or for a misdemeanor, and prior to conviction, be fined under this title or imprisoned not more than one year, or both.

(b) Whoever escapes or attempts to escape from the custody of the Attorney General or his authorized representative, or from any institution or facility in which he is confined by direction of the Attorney General, or from any custody under or by virtue of any process issued under the laws of the United States by any court, judge, or magistrate judge, or from the custody of an officer or employee of the United States pursuant to lawful arrest, shall, if the custody or confinement is by virtue of a lawful arrest for a violation of any law of the United States not punishable by death or life imprisonment and committed before such person's eighteenth birthday, and as to whom the Attorney General has not specifically directed the institution of criminal proceedings, or by virtue of a commitment as a juvenile delinquent under section 5034 of this title, be fined under this title or imprisoned not more than one year, or both. Nothing herein contained shall be construed to affect the discretionary authority vested in the Attorney General pursuant to section 5032 of this title.

court can accept the plea agreement and agree to the joint sentencing recommendation, or it can reject the entire plea agreement. If the court accepts the plea agreement, it is bound by the recommendation—in Duke's case, that the sentence of imprisonment not exceed 15 years.

The joint sentencing recommendation reflected the extent of Duke's cooperation. Without this plea agreement, Duke would have faced a sentence of 30 years—the maximum sentence allowed under the statute.

SENTENCING

In federal cases, sentences are determined by applying the relevant statute—in this case, 18 U.S.C. § 3553(a)—and the United States Sentencing Guidelines. While the Sentencing Guidelines are advisory, the judge who determines the sentence must first calculate the sentencing range under the Guidelines. The Guidelines seek to quantify the criminal conduct in order to calculate an appropriate sentence, taking into consideration the harm caused by the crime, the defendant's role in the offense, the number of victims, and other aggravating and mitigating circumstances. After the offense conduct is calculated, the defendant's criminal history is scored and categorized. These two scores—the offense conduct level and the criminal history category—determine the advisory sentencing range on the Sentencing Table (USSG, § 5A).

Under the Sentencing Guidelines, the base offense for conspiracy to commit wire fraud is level 7 (USSG § 2B1.1). The government's estimate of the loss was more than $100 million, which adds an additional twenty-six levels to that base (USSG § 2B1.1(b)(1)(N)). Duke argued that the loss was between $50 million and $100 million, which would add twenty-four levels.

In addition, this was a crime that involved sophisticated means, which the Guidelines define as "especially complex or especially intricate offense conduct pertaining to the execution or concealment of an offense" (USSG § 2B1.1(b)(9)(C), since renumbered as § 2B1.1(b)(10(C)). This added two levels. The Guidelines also consider the number of victims, which the government maintained exceeded fifty and which, if proven, would add another four levels (USSG § 2B1.1(b)(2)(B)). Duke argued that there were between ten and forty-nine victims, resulting in only a two-level increase (USSG § 2B1.1(b)(2) (A)). Because Duke was a leader and organizer of the criminal enterprise, and the scheme involved more than five participants, four levels were added (USSG § 3B1.1(a)).

By pleading guilty, Duke received three levels off for acceptance of responsibility (USSG § 3E1.1).

The government's estimate of Duke's total offense level was 40. Duke's lawyers estimated he was at level 36. The parties agreed that his criminal history put him in Criminal History Category IV. Under the government's estimate, that would put his advisory sentencing range at 30 years to life imprisonment. Under Duke's estimate, he faced between 22 and 27 years.

The above Guidelines analysis may seem a meaningless exercise since the government and the defendant agreed on a sentencing range, but the law directs the sentencing judge to correctly calculate the offense level per the Guidelines as the first step in determining a proper sentence. Arriving at that advisory sentencing range also shows how much the recommended sentence departs from the Guidelines. And it illustrates the value that the government placed on Duke's cooperation. In this case, it showed that Duke was getting a huge break—15 years or more off his sentence—in return for his help.

Prior to the sentencing hearing, prosecutors and Duke's attorneys continued to fight over the loss amount and the number of victims. In addition, the plea agreement had underestimated Duke's criminal history. The presentence investigation found that he fell into Category VI, the highest category on the Sentencing Table, with prior convictions for embezzlement, receiving and concealing stolen property, credit card fraud, malicious use of a telecommunication service to threaten, escape, and aggravated stalking (Government's Sentencing Memorandum, 2013).

By the time Duke came before the court to learn his fate, the fifteen other defendants involved in the scheme had pleaded guilty and been sentenced. The government identified seven other individuals who had assisted Duke. The other defendants were sentenced to terms that ranged from 8 to 10 years. Duke's willingness to testify likely induced others to plead guilty.

Duke's usefulness as a trial witness, however, was undermined by his behavior during the time he was working with the government. He sent emails to an FBI agent in which he made racist and sexist remarks about some of his codefendants. Those materials were provided to those codefendants' attorneys as *Brady* material and likely would have been the subject of his cross-examination.[1]

The government also noted that Duke's assistance was offset by his belated objection to some of the disputed losses. But eventually, the United States agreed to compromise on the Guideline dispute, conceding that there were forty victims, all mortgage lenders, and that the total loss amounted to just under $95 million (Government's Supplemental Sentencing Memorandum, 2013). Considering all of Duke's cooperation and assistance, the prosecutors requested that the court impose a sentence in the range of 156 to 180 months, that is, between 13 and 15 years. Prosecutors asked that Duke, who had been on pretrial release since his arrest, be immediately taken into custody at the sentencing hearing.

At Duke's sentencing on April 8, 2013, the defense argued for a sentence of no more than 10 years, on the grounds that the loss amount was less than originally thought. Duke's attorneys also argued that Duke's sentence should be comparable to the terms imposed on his codefendants, who faced sentences of no more than 10 years (Transcript, Sentencing Hearing, 2013, p. 9). Under 18 U.S.C. § 3553(a)(6), the sentencing judge must "avoid unwarranted sentence disparities among defendants with similar records who have been found guilty of similar conduct."

At a sentencing hearing, the defendant is permitted, but not required, to make a statement prior to being sentenced, a process called *allocution*. Duke took the opportunity to apologize for his conduct (Transcript, Sentencing

---

1. The Supreme Court's decision in *Brady v. Maryland,* 373 U.S. 83 (1963), established that the prosecution must turn over to the defense all evidence that might exonerate the defendant (exculpatory evidence).

Hearing, 2013, p. 47). He told the court that once he met with his attorney and decided to cooperate with the government, he had immediately begun taking steps to downsize his business, but not so much that it would alert his coschemers. He detailed his surreptitious recording of his coconspirators and extensive work with the FBI. And he pointed out that he had immediately forfeited $1.4 million in assets that had been purchased using his profits from the fraud. Duke expressed his remorse for his "greed and stupidity" (Transcript, Sentencing Hearing, 2013, p. 48). His admiration for the FBI agents with whom he had worked, he said, had led him to enroll in college and seek a degree in criminal justice.

Due to his history of substance abuse, Duke asked to the judge to recommend that he participate in a drug treatment program. The Residential Drug Abuse Program (RDAP) permits inmates to take up to a year off their sentence if they successfully complete the five-hundred-hour treatment program. Because there is no parole in the federal system, defendants must serve 85 percent of their sentence, and at the time, RDAP was one of the few ways to earn time off of a prison sentence. Duke also asked the court to let him self-surrender to prison so he'd have time to get his affairs in order.

The prosecutor agreed that Duke's cooperation was extraordinary for a defendant in such a significant case. This defendant's situation was unusual in that Duke, the lead organizer of the scheme, had cooperated with the government. That circumstance, and the scope of the nearly $100 million scheme, convinced the prosecutor that "this is not a case where the Guidelines are necessarily that helpful to us because they are just so high" (Transcript, Sentencing Hearing, 2013, p. 67).

Prosecutors objected to the characterization of the 13- to 15-year sentence as disproportionate to the codefendants' sentences by arguing that "there was no question that Mr. Duke was at the top of that hierarchy" (Transcript, Sentencing Hearing, 2013, p. 67). Prosecutors argued that any difference between the sentences of Duke and his codefendants was due to Duke's more extensive criminal history. And while it was commendable that Duke was going back to school, the prosecutor noted that he had taken out $24,000 worth of student loans to pay for his college courses and it was unclear how he intended to repay that debt, in light of his pending prison sentence (Transcript, Sentencing Hearing, 2013, p. 70).

After considering the sentencing factors set forth in 18 USC § 3553(a), Judge Julian Abele Cook Jr. sentenced Duke to 13 years in prison, followed by 5 years of supervised release. The judge also imposed a $1 million fine and ordered Duke to repay $94 million in restitution to the lenders who had submitted claims. He recommended that Duke participate in the drug treatment program, and over prosecutors' objections, he permitted Duke to remain out on bond until June 3, 2013, when he would report to prison.

AFTERMATH

Duke was ordered to serve his sentence at the Federal Correctional Facility Gilmer in Glenville, West Virginia. But on June 3, 2013, Duke did not appear to self-surrender at the prison, and the court issued a warrant for his arrest.

Duke was a fugitive until February 24, 2014, when he was arrested by U.S. marshals. He was charged with one count of failure to surrender for sentence, a violation of 18 U.S.C. § 3146(a)(2) (Superseding Indictment, 2014). While Duke was in custody, jail officials found that he had removed the mortar in the cinderblock wall near the window of his cell. Prosecutors added a charge of attempted escape from federal custody, a violation of 18 U.S.C. § 751(a).

Even this was not the end of Duke's legal drama. At his first court appearance after he was arrested, Duke lunged at the federal prosecutor, grabbed her by the hair, and struck her in the face (Transcript, Sentencing Hearing, April 8, 2016, p. 52). He was then charged in a separate indictment with assaulting a federal employee, a violation of 18 U.S.C. § 111. Because the victim of the assault was a prosecutor in the Eastern District of Michigan, none of the attorneys in that office could handle the case. Instead, two assistant United States attorneys from the Northern District of Ohio were appointed to prosecute him on the assault charge.

Duke pleaded guilty without a plea agreement to the assault charge. He was sentenced on April 8, 2016, three years to the day after his last sentencing hearing on the mortgage fraud conviction. While his assault and escape cases were pending, Duke was diagnosed with bipolar disorder and he began treatment (Transcript, Sentencing Hearing, April 8, 2016). At sentencing, he again apologized and said that after his diagnosis and through his ongoing treatment, he could look back and see his erratic behavior.

"I don't go buy one Corvette, I go buy three Corvettes," he told the court (Transcript, Sentencing Hearing, April 8, 2016, p. 44). When he was in a manic state, which he called his Superman state, "everything's great, you can do anything. . . . I used to race my race car, fly a helicopter . . . the sky is the limit. But then you start going the other way—you just turn into somebody you don't want to be" (Transcript, Sentencing Hearing, 2016, p. 45).

Duke also apologized to the prosecutor whom he had attacked. She was not present, but had submitted a victim impact statement, in which she said that she had suffered not only physical injury but also emotional scars from being assaulted while doing her job.

The prosecutors and defense attorney argued over Duke's previous criminal history, as well as the applicable Guidelines, and Judge Stephen J. Murphy determined that a range of 78 to 97 months was the appropriate sentencing range and that Duke was in Criminal History Category III. Because of the passage of time, some of his older criminal convictions were no longer considered. Judge Murphy imposed a sentence of 97 months, a little more than 8 years', imprisonment, the high end of the Guideline range, because this was "an extreme case of anger, violence and viciousness unleashed" (Transcript, Sentencing Hearing, April 8, 2016, p. 59). The assault sentence would run consecutive to the 13-year mortgage fraud prison sentence.

Two weeks later, on April 22, 2016, Duke was sentenced on the charges of failure to appear and attempted escape (Transcript, Sentencing Hearing, April 22, 2016). In this case, he did have a plea agreement, in which he pleaded guilty to both counts. Both sides agreed that the sentence should be between 18 and 24 months. For the third time, Duke addressed the court and apologized for his conduct. He again stressed that he was learning to take his mental health seriously, was on medication, and was participating in group and one-on-one counseling. He promised to continue to work on his mental health and to strive to be a better man. He asked to be housed in a program that would permit him to continue with his mental health treatment.

Judge Murphy noted that between the mortgage fraud sentence and the assault sentence, Duke would be imprisoned for 23 years (Transcript, Sentencing Hearing, April 22, 2016, p. 11). He noted that Duke's allocution appeared sincere.

"I just can't find it within myself to tack on an extra two years. With the amount of work this man has to do, twenty-three years I think should be sufficient to punish him for everything he did in the mortgage fraud case, everything he did in the assault case, and the nature of the conviction plus the additional conditions ... will hopefully punish him, cause a lack of recidivism, deter him and others," Judge Murphy said (Transcript, Sentencing Hearing, April 22, 2016, p. 11). The judge found that Duke had been mentally ill when he engaged in all of the crimes. "Maybe he's misleading me, I don't think he is, maybe he's misleading me, (but) it seems he's turned the corner in terms of learning about his mental health and trying to address it. . . . I think if we encourage him by imposing a just but not overly harsh sentence here, that will hopefully help him on his way" (Transcript, Sentencing Hearing, April 22, 2016, p. 11).

Judge Murphy sentenced Duke to 18 months on the two counts that run concurrent with each other and with the assault sentence.

POSTSCRIPT

After all this, Ronnie Duke's legal troubles were not yet over.

In 2017, the federal government charged Duke with nine counts of wire fraud for allegedly committing financial fraud while he was on pretrial release in the first fraud case (Indictment, 2017). Prosecutors said that Duke used a fake name to lure investors into a real estate improvement program that involved the investors applying for new lines of credit. Duke then allegedly used shell companies to withdraw funds against that credit. The indictment charged that Duke obtained $3.5 million through this scheme, and made less than $15,000 in actual purchases that could be construed as housing or home improvement costs. In addition to the wire fraud charges, he was charged with committing this offense while on pretrial release, a violation of 18 U.S.C. § 3147. Duke pleaded not guilty and the case was pending as of 2020.

REFERENCES

Annual Statistical Report. (2012). United States Attorneys' Annual Statistical Report.

Annual Statistical Report. (2017). United States Attorneys' Annual Statistical Report.

Financial Crisis Inquiry Commission. (2011). *The Financial Crisis Inquiry Report: Final Report of the National Commission on the Causes of the Financial and Economic Crisis in the United States.* Washington, DC.

PSI Report. (2011). Permanent Subcommittee on Investigations, Committee on Homeland Security and Governmental Affairs, United States Senate. *Wall Street and the Financial Crisis: Anatomy of a Financial Collapse.* https://www .hsgac.senate.gov//imo/media/doc/Financial_Crisis/FinancialCrisisReport.pdf? attempt=2.

COURT DOCUMENTS (BY CHARGE)

Mortgage Fraud (11-cr-20017)

Complaint. (2010). United State v. Duke, Case No. 11-cr-20017. E. Dist. Michigan. June 16.

Government's Sentencing Memorandum. (2013). United States v. Duke, 11-cr-20017-JAC-VMM. E. Dist. Michigan. January 31.

Government's Supplemental Sentencing Memorandum. (2013). United States v. Duke, 11-cr-20017-JAC-VMM. E. Dist. Michigan. April 2.

Plea Agreement. (2012). United States v. Duke, 11-cr-20017-JAC-VMM. E. Dist. Michigan. July 6.

Transcript, Sentencing Hearing. (2013). United States v. Duke, 11-cr-20017-JAC-VMM. E. Dist. Michigan. April 8.

Failure to Appear, Escape (13-cr-20881)

Superseding Indictment. (2014). United States v. Duke, 13-cr-20881-SJM-MKM. E. Dist. Michigan. August 7.

Transcript, Sentencing Hearing. (April 22, 2016). United States v. Duke, 13-cr-20881. E. Dist. Michigan. April 22.

Assault (14-cr-20136)

Transcript, Sentencing Hearing. (2016). United States v. Duke, 14-cr-20136. E. Dist. Michigan. Transcript, Sentencing Hearing. April 8.

Wire Fraud (17-cr-20733)

Indictment. (2017). United States v. Ronnie Duke, 17-cr-20733. E. Dist. Michigan. November 1.

THREE

Ponzi Schemes

UTAH V. DEE RANDALL

IT WASN'T EASY TO CHOOSE a case to illustrate Ponzi schemes. There were just so many options.

Since this type of criminal fraud scheme first entered the public consciousness, it has become distressingly common. Most often, Ponzi schemes promise investors high returns not available through traditional investments. But instead of investing the funds, the promoter pays "dividends" to initial investors using the funds of subsequent investors. The schemes generally collapse when the operators flee with the proceeds or when the scheme's organizer runs out of new investors and can't continue paying previous victims.

Though he wasn't the first to hatch such a scheme, Boston businessman Charles Ponzi's crime gave this type of fraud its name. In 1919, Ponzi promised investors a 50 percent return on a ninety-day investment in international postal coupons (Frankel, 2012). He paid his initial investors with money from latecomers to the scheme, but soon became unable to pay out the later investors.

It's the same scheme that Bernie Madoff ran for decades—though Madoff's was on a far larger scale (Frankel, 2012). For at least thirty years, investors in Madoff's hedge fund thought they were earning steady returns averaging 11 percent annually on their investments. In reality, their funds were being used to pay other investors' dividends and to fund Madoff's lifestyle. Madoff's elite clients received statements that showed their investments were growing at a steady rate, but those gains were false. In 2008, when the financial markets tumbled, investors sought to withdraw $7 billion—far more than Madoff had available. The scheme collapsed, Madoff was arrested, and investors lost an estimated $50 billion in purported earnings. Madoff pleaded guilty and was sentenced to 150 years in federal prison. His investors have recovered $12.8 billion, about 73 percent of the lost principal invested, as of December 2017.

Ponzi schemes take many forms, but are commonly seen in brokerage situations. Sometimes a legitimate brokerage runs into financial trouble, and the fraud begins as a way to temporarily pay dividends, then grows out of control. Other times, the brokerage firm is created solely for the purpose of defrauding victims. Ponzi schemes are unsustainable and offer few exit strategies for the organizers. The structure requires an ever-increasing supply of new money to maintain payments to prior investors, not to mention paying the promoter. Once the promoter fails to find a sufficient number of new investors to cover payments owed to the prior investors, the scheme collapses.

It's not an accident that the Ponzi scheme in this case study is from Utah. The Beehive State routinely ranks at or near the top of states frequently targeted by scammers (Harvey, 2011). A study by Marquet International looked at the percentage of Ponzi fraud schemes per state, divided by the state's percentage of the nation's gross domestic product (Marquet International Ltd., 2011). Utah ranked tenth for the number of schemes totaling more than $1 million. And it ranked ninth as a percentage of the total number of cases.

Utah residents are also frequent victims of affinity fraud. These cases involve schemes where the perpetrator targets those who share common interests and emotional ties, such as a church affiliation. Affinity fraud exploits the trust people have in those who share their faith, their ethnic background, or another common interest. Utah lawmakers recognized the state had a fraud problem and in 2015 enacted the nation's first white-collar crime registry, Stop Fraud Utah (Utah Office of the Attorney General, 2018). Using a model similar to those for sex offenders, Utah requires that those convicted of fraud be listed in a public, online registry that includes a photo of the offender and a brief summary of their crime (Protess, 2015). Offenses on the registry include securities fraud, mortgage fraud, and money laundering. First-time offenders are listed for ten years. Those convicted of a third offense will remain on the registry for life.

The case study in this chapter illustrates many of the commonly seen traits seen in Ponzi schemes; there are elements of affinity fraud and of a failed brokerage. Unlike most of the other cases in this book, this one was prosecuted in state court. But there are sufficient elements that the case against Dee Allen Randall could have been brought in federal court.

Andrew Dean Kelley

Sentenced in October 2017 to 7 years in federal prison and ordered to pay $8 million in restitution. Kelley told his investors that he had developed sophisticated trading software that had generated a 300 percent return the first year he used it. He also played up his devotion to the LDS Church. Prosecutors estimate that eighty-four investors lost more than $12 million.[1]

Curtis DeYoung

Sentenced to 10 years in federal prison. Prosecutors alleged that DeYoung's investors lost $25 million that they'd transferred from their retirement accounts. In sentencing DeYoung, the judge noted that fraud was epidemic in the community. There is "an inexhaustible supply of gullible victims and predators," he said.[2]

Lori Ann Anderson

Sentenced to 2 to 30 years in state prison in January 2016. She pled guilty to defrauding forty-six investors out of more than $1.7 million in a day-trading scam. It was her second conviction for fraud. The Utah Division of Securities said Anderson's victims handed over "their trust and money in a church environment."[3]

John Scott Clark

Sentenced to 3 years in federal prison in April 2016. According to a Securities and Exchange Commission complaint, Clark solicited members of his church, promising astronomical returns on their

---

1. Hunt, S. (2017). "Utah Man Sentenced to Prison for Fraud Scheme That Took Millions from Investors." *Salt Lake Tribune,* October 5.

2. Harvey, T. (2016). "Victims Upset Draper Man Gets Only 10 Years in Prison for Stealing $25 Million in Retirement Funds. *Salt Lake Tribune,* November 22.

3. Noble, M. (2016). "Utah Woman Sentenced Gets Prison for a Second Round of Defrauding Investors." *Salt Lake Tribune,* May 24.

THE CASE

Dee Allen Randall was the picture of a successful businessman. A licensed
broker-dealer agent in the state of Utah since 1987, he had successfully completed the Series 6, 22, and 63 exams, which enabled him to sell certain types
of securities. From 1996 to 2011, Randall was employed as the general agent
in Utah for Union Central Life Insurance, a Nebraska-based life insurance
company, and he had offices in several Utah cities. He employed numerous
others who worked in those offices under his license (Harvey, 2015). Randall
and his sales agents pitched life insurance and other financial products to a
community that trusted Randall because of his reputation in the insurance
community and because of his standing in the Church of Jesus Christ of
Latter-day Saints (LDS Church).

In 1996, Randall established several companies, including Horizon
Financial and Insurance Group, Inc.; Horizon Auto Funding, LLC;
Independent Commercial Lending, LLC; and Independent Property
Management, LLC (Complaint, 2014). Randall was also the owner of
Horizon Mortgage and Investment. Through his companies, Randall offered
"Horizon Notes," promissory notes with annual returns of between 9 and
17 percent. Investors' money would be pooled to finance car loans and real
estate development.

The promissory notes for Horizon Auto Funding, which provided subprime loans for autos, were sold as an opportunity to earn a 14 percent annual
return, secured by car titles, with a minimum investment of $100,000 (OSC,
2012). The investment was safe, Randall assured his clients, because even in a
bad economy everyone needs cars and the investment would fail only "if the

whole country went down" (OSC, 2012, p. 16). Investors would receive monthly payments from Horizon Auto until the principal was repaid. To get in on this opportunity, some of Randall's clients withdrew their retirement funds or tapped into the equity in their homes.

Randall also provided opportunities to invest in residential and commercial property development, through another of his companies, Independent Financial and Investment. These investments were offered as *private placement offerings,* which are securities not sold in a public offering. In total, through the various entities he owned, controlled, or operated, Randall raised more than $72 million from approximately seven hundred investors.

Randall's success came via word of mouth and from his agents and clients and focused on working people and retirees, many of whom knew Randall or knew of his reputation through the LDS Church.

Chip Lyons, an analyst with the Division of Securities of the Utah Department of Commerce, said that Randall was trusted by his clients because of his standing in the community and his church (personal communication, October 16, 2018). "The affinity angle was a crucial part of his ability to gain additional investors," Lyons said. "We were aware of an instance where a widow and her children met with him and there was a prayer at the beginning of the meeting."

With a retired couple, Randall played on his church affiliation to persuade the two to invest, said Dave Hermansen, director of enforcement for the Utah Division of Securities (personal communication, October 16, 2018). "He went to their house and did the solicitation, but then let them know that he had to run over to the temple and be in a ceremony." That shared moral foundation gave him a veneer of familiarity and trustworthiness, Hermansen said. "People trusted him because they shared a faith."

Randall disclosed to some of his investors in a private-placement memorandum that their money would be used to pay what was due to earlier investors. He also warned that investors should not invest money that they could not afford to lose.

What those investors did not know, and what Randall did not disclose, was that he had not been licensed to sell securities since 1997, and that he had stopped making payments to investors in 2009. He filed for bankruptcy in December 2010, another fact that was not disclosed to investors.

The first complaints to the Utah Division of Securities about Randall and his agents arrived in 2009, after Randall began defaulting on the Horizon Note payments. He filed for Chapter 11 bankruptcy in December 2010, and the state securities division opened a formal investigation into his businesses six months later.

After filing for bankruptcy, Randall continued to solicit investments and raised $1.6 million from thirty-five investors. A trustee was appointed to manage the bankruptcy estate for three of Randall's companies, which he sought to reorganize and continue to operate (Harvey, 2015). After a thorough review of the companies, the trustee found that the businesses had been insolvent since at least 1997.

Randall had an interesting defense to the allegation that his businesses were incapable of paying the promised returns except by using funds from new investors. Because he had told investors he was going to use their money to repay earlier investors, he argued that such a disclosure got around the security laws—that the investment was in effect a legal Ponzi scheme. The Utah Division of Securities disagreed, countering that there's no such thing as legal fraud.

"Using money from new investors to pay older investors, with no way to generate profits to pay people back, is a fraud regardless of whether you disclose it or not," said Keith Woodwell, then director of the Utah Division of Securities (Harvey, 2015).

THE PROSECUTION

In June 2014, Randall was charged with twenty-two counts of felony securities fraud. Some of the charges were enhanced because the investors had used funds withdrawn from retirement accounts. The state also alleged that Randall's operation constituted a pattern of unlawful activity, a violation of Utah Code Annotated § 76-10-1601, also a felony charge (see sidebar 3.2).

The Utah Division of Securities investigated the case. In the affidavit of probable cause supporting the criminal complaint, the agency noted a history of red flags in Randall's businesses, including a 2002 violation of state and federal securities laws for issuing unregistered securities. Randall's companies operated as a Ponzi scheme, the government said, in which investors'

§ 61-1-1. Fraud unlawful.

It is unlawful for any person, in connection with the offer, sale, or purchase of any security, directly or indirectly to:

(1) employ any device, scheme or artifice to defraud;

(2) make any untrue statement of a material fact or to omit to state a material fact necessary in order to make the statement made, in the light of the circumstances under which they are made, not misleading; or

(3) engage in any act, practice, or course of business which operates or would operate as a fraud or deceit upon any person.

§ 61-1-21. Penalties for violations.

(1) A person is guilty of a third-degree felony who willfully violates:
   (a) a provision of this chapter except Sections 61-1-1 and 61-1-16;
   (b) an order issued under this chapter; or
   (c) Section 61-1-16 knowing the statement made is false or misleading in a material respect.

(2) Subject to the other provisions of this section, a person who willfully violates Section 61-1-1:
   (a) is guilty of a third-degree felony if, at the time the crime was committed, the property, money, or thing unlawfully obtained or sought to be obtained was worth less than $10,000; or
   (b) is guilty of a second-degree felony if, at the time the crime was committed, the property, money, or thing unlawfully obtained or sought to be obtained was worth $10,000 or more.

(3) A person who willfully violates Section 61-1-1 is guilty of a second degree felony if:
   (a) at the time the crime was committed, the property, money, or thing unlawfully obtained or sought to be obtained was worth less than $10,000; and
   (b) in connection with that violation, the violator knowingly accepted any money representing:
      (i) equity in a person's primary residence;

    (ii) a withdrawal from an individual retirement account;

    (iii) a withdrawal from a qualified retirement plan as defined in the Internal Revenue Code;

    (iv) an investment by a person over whom the violator exercises undue influence; or

    (v) an investment by a person that the violator knows is a vulnerable adult.

(4) A person who willfully violates Section 61-1-1 is guilty of a second degree felony punishable by imprisonment for an indeterminate term of not less than three years or more than 15 years if:

  (a) at the time the crime was committed, the property, money, or thing unlawfully obtained or sought to be obtained was worth $10,000 or more; and

  (b) in connection with that violation, the violator knowingly accepted any money representing:

    (i) equity in a person's primary residence;

    (ii) a withdrawal from an individual retirement account;

    (iii) a withdrawal from a qualified retirement plan as defined in the Internal Revenue Code;

    (iv) an investment by a person over whom the violator exercises undue influence; or

    (v) an investment by a person that the violator knows is a vulnerable adult.

(5) When amounts of property, money, or other things are unlawfully obtained or sought to be obtained under a series of acts or continuing course of business, whether from the same or several sources, the amounts may be aggregated in determining the level of offense.

(6) It is an affirmative defense under this section against a claim that the person violated an order issued under this chapter for the person to prove that the person had no knowledge of the order.

(7) In addition to any other penalty for a criminal violation of this chapter, the sentencing judge may impose a penalty or remedy provided for in Subsection 61-1-20(2)(b).

§ 76-10-1603. Unlawful acts.

(1) It is unlawful for any person who has received any proceeds derived, whether directly or indirectly, from a pattern of unlawful

activity in which the person has participated as a principal, to use or invest, directly or indirectly, any part of that income, or the proceeds of the income, or the proceeds derived from the investment or use of those proceeds, in the acquisition of any interest in, or the establishment or operation of, any enterprise.

(2) It is unlawful for any person through a pattern of unlawful activity to acquire or maintain, directly or indirectly, any interest in or control of any enterprise.

(3) It is unlawful for any person employed by or associated with any enterprise to conduct or participate, whether directly or indirectly, in the conduct of that enterprise's affairs through a pattern of unlawful activity.

(4) It is unlawful for any person to conspire to violate any provision of Subsection (1), (2), or (3).

§ 76-10-1602. Definitions.

As used in this part:

(1) "Enterprise" means any individual, sole proprietorship, partnership, corporation, business trust, association, or other legal entity, and any union or group of individuals associated in fact although not a legal entity, and includes illicit as well as licit entities.

(2) "Pattern of unlawful activity" means engaging in conduct which constitutes the commission of at least three episodes of unlawful activity, which episodes are not isolated, but have the same or similar purposes, results, participants, victims, or methods of commission, or otherwise are interrelated by distinguishing characteristics. Taken together, the episodes shall demonstrate continuing unlawful conduct and be related either to each other or to the enterprise. At least one of the episodes comprising a pattern of unlawful activity shall have occurred after July 31, 1981. The most recent act constituting part of a pattern of unlawful activity as defined by this part shall have occurred within five years of the commission of the next preceding act alleged as part of the pattern.

. . .

(4) "Unlawful activity" means to directly engage in conduct or to solicit, request, command, encourage, or intentionally aid

money was routinely and freely commingled and transferred among the various Horizon entities. Some of the new investor monies were paid to prior
investors, or to "financial advisors" and insurance sales agents in sales compensation. Most of the sales agents were not licensed to sell securities or did
not have approval from the broker-dealer or investment advisor they were
affiliated with to offer the Horizon Notes (Hermansen Affidavit, 2014).

"The problem with every Ponzi scheme is that you need a constant influx
of new money," Chip Lyons said. Randall pushed his agents to sell whole-life
policies, which require higher monthly payments. Then the agent would sell
a promissory note that would generate enough income to cover that monthly
payment.

The insurance policies also paid significant up-front commissions to
Randall's office, giving him that income as well. But, if the client stopped
paying on the insurance policy within a year, the agent would have to repay
the commission. Randall made sure to make the payments on the promissory
notes so that the clients could cover their life insurance payments—and his
agency could thrive in the insurance industry, "getting vacation incentives
and awards," bolstering his reputation, Lyons said.

Initially, Randall had told his insurance agents they could not sell Horizon
Notes themselves, because they were not licensed to sell securities. Instead,
Randall encouraged them to refer prospective investors directly to him. In some
cases, the sales agents brought clients to meet with Randall, who would then
explain the investment opportunities available in the various Horizon entities.

Investigators uncovered overwhelming evidence that, despite Randall's
directive, the agents were regularly selling Horizon Notes. Starting in 2007,

Randall began paying sales agents in Utah and Idaho a commission of 1 percent based on the investors' principle investment. Two years later, Randall changed the commission structure to 7 percent for closing an investment of more than $50,000, and 10 percent for investments below that amount. Randall paid cash to the agents or would disguise the compensation as allowances for office space rental, insurance, marketing, or credits against money owed to Randall.

This went on for two decades. Some of Randall's business was legitimate, but, as Lyons observed, "the more investors you take in, the more pressure you have to make payments."

Randall's accountant told investigators that he believed the company took in between $50 million and $65 million over fifteen years, but the business never generated sufficient real income to cover its contractually obligated interest payments on the notes (Hermansen Affidavit, 2014). The company's accounting firm issued "going concern" opinions from 2003 through 2006—meaning that the accountant had substantial doubt about the company's ability to continue to operate. When investors started calling the accounting firm's office for information in 2008, the accountant became aware that Randall had been missing payments or making late payments. Randall prioritized payments based on who complained the most, who had their attorneys send letters, or who filed lawsuits. By late 2009 or early 2010, the accountant was aware that new investor funds were being diverted to pay previous obligations. Randall had begun to miss interest payments around 2005.

The Division of Securities investigation found that Randall failed to provide investors a private-placement memorandum, a document that outlines investment risk, use of the proceeds, management experience, disclosures, financial statements, and other information that permits investors to make informed decisions. He also did not disclose that he was paying sales agents for referrals for sales. After he filed for bankruptcy in December 2010, he did not disclose this material information to the investors.

Investors often put their entire retirement fund or life savings into Randall's companies, and some took out equity from their homes to invest. Some investors used money they received from life insurance policies upon the death of loved ones. As a result, many investors lost their entire retirement savings, homes, or insurance policies because they were unable to make payments once Randall stopped paying interest checks on the Horizon Notes.

The widow who had invested her children's college fund "was one of the hardest hit," said Enforcement Director Hermansen. There were many similar stories. Though the twenty-two separate fraud charges each addressed a different transaction, the complaint did not include every fraudulent sale. The last charge in the complaint, however, alleged a pattern of unlawful activity, which requires a minimum of three instances of securities fraud and can encompass the entire scheme. The total scope of Randall's criminal operation, prosecutors alleged, involved more than $72 million from some seven hundred investors through April 2011.

SENTENCING

Randall pleaded guilty to four counts of securities fraud and one count of a pattern of unlawful activity (Plea Agreement, 2016). In his plea agreement, he admitted making untrue statements of material fact or omitting material information to obtain money by deceit. The state sought restitution in the amount of $36.8 million, though it left the final calculation of the loss to the court. The plea agreement specified that the defendant understood that by pleading guilty he would be listed on the Utah White-Collar Crime Registry for 10 years.

At the sentencing hearing in February 2017, several investors told the court what the loss had done to them. But the delay between the discovery of the fraud and the imposition of the sentence caused some victims, Lyons noted, to soften their stance.

"It was amazing to see how they backed off wanting him to die in jail, instead saying it wasn't their place to judge him," Lyons said. "None of them were saying he was a crook, he stole their money, and I hope you go to prison for the rest of your life. Many had to go back to work. They didn't have malice in their hearts for that guy."

"As someone who felt strongly about this case, it made me very nervous listening to those people in court," Lyons recalled.

Randall was sentenced to consecutive prison terms on three counts of securities fraud, which were enhanced because they involved retirement funds, resulting in a sentence of 9 to 30 years in prison. He was also sentenced to concurrent sentences for one count of securities fraud, a 3- to 15-year term, and one count of engaging in a pattern of unlawful activity, a sentence of 1 to 15 years (Minutes, Sentencing Hearing, 2017). The sentence— up to 30 years—was one of the longest imposed for a white-collar crime in Utah.

About forty victims and family members attended Randall's sentencing hearing. Randall addressed the court and asked for leniency and a chance to work and repay some of what he owed the victims.

"I am deeply sorry for every single investor," Randall said (Lockhart, 2017). He added that he had not had a day in several years in which he hadn't felt heartache over the fate of those who invested their money with him. "I know that doesn't do them any good."

Randall was immediately taken into custody at the end of the hearing.

AFTERMATH

While the criminal case was resolved with Randall's guilty plea, the legal system continued to work to make the victims whole. As part of the sentence in the criminal case, Randall was ordered to pay restitution to the victims. Since he was 66 years old when he was sentenced to a term of between 9 and 30 years, it was unlikely that he would be able to earn any significant income.

The bankruptcy trustee continued to consolidate assets to repay victims and to settle a $1.2 million debt with the Internal Revenue Service, and pursued legal action against the insurance company affiliated with Randall's business. In January 2019, the bankruptcy trustee filed a final report and asked the court to close the case. In the final accounting, approximately $25 million was distributed from the bankruptcy estate (Trustee's Final Report, 2019).

The Utah Division of Securities investigated several agents for and employees of Randall's businesses, and brought civil actions against eleven agents. One agent was charged criminally and pleaded guilty to one count of attempted securities fraud, a misdemeanor.

CHALLENGES OF INVESTIGATING PONZI SCHEMES

For Chris Lyons and Dave Hermansen, the Randall case illustrated the difficulty of detecting and investigating Ponzi schemes—for both regulators and consumers.

Fraud statutes generally have a 5-year statute of limitation for criminal charges, but Ponzi scheme operators engage in "lulling behavior," paying victims their scheduled dividends to give the appearance of legitimacy. In Randall's case, it was a challenge to find cooperating investors who had been harmed and to whom false representations had been made during that statute of limitations, Lyons noted.

A key tactic in establishing the existence of a Ponzi scheme, Hermansen observed, is to "follow the money." Securities regulators spend a lot of time going through bank records and tracking transfers between accounts. But investigators don't subpoena those records unless a victim comes forward—and due to the lulling payments, those people may not know they are victims for years.

For consumers, the Utah White-Collar Crime Registry is a new tool for combatting fraud, but it has its limitations, Hermansen said. The registry lists those convicted of a second-degree felony and includes a photograph and a brief description of the crime. But often defendants can have their conviction reduced to a third-degree felony or a misdemeanor by paying court-ordered restitution. At that point, they drop off the registry. In cases where the case is resolved with a civil agreement, they never appear on the registry in the first place.

Investors who are considering an investment sales pitch can call their state securities regulators to get more information about the person selling the investment opportunity. That will at least show whether the person is licensed and in good standing, or if they've had been disciplined by regulators in the past. Potential investors can request audited financial statements and then verify that information with the accountant who prepared the audit, Lyons said.

And there's no overstating the importance of thinking critically about investment opportunities. Investors should research typical rates of return, and if a prospective deal pays far more, ask why. "Consumers should ask, 'What are they doing that banks can't do?'" Hermansen advised.

Despite all the consumer education, fraud registries, and high-profile cases investigated and prosecuted, there will always be a need to police the financial industry.

People are trusting, Lyons said, and "all humans have a certain element of greed, of thinking that if you're living well, good things will come to you."

This prosperity thinking allows hopeful investors to imagine that a new opportunity that had just dropped in front of them is that reward. "There are always crafty people," Lyons said. "You can never stop a new Ponzi scheme."

Complaint. (2014). Utah v. Randall, Case No. 141906717 FS. Third Judicial District, Salt Lake County, State of Utah. June 18.

Frankel, T. (2012). *The Ponzi Scheme Puzzle*. New York: Oxford University Press.

Harvey, T. (2011). "Utah Named a Top Ponzi State—Again." *Salt Lake Tribune*. June 29.

Harvey, T. (2015). "Utah Judge Rules that 'Legal' Ponzi Scheme, Targeted to Mormons, Was Still Just Fraud." *Salt Lake Tribune,* March 28.

Hermansen Affidavit. (2014). Utah v. Randall, No. 141906717. Third Judicial District, Salt Lake County, State of Utah. Hermansen, D., Affidavit of Probable Cause. June 18.

Lockhart, B. (2017). "'The Damage Is Done': Man behind One of Utah's Largest Ponzi Schemes Gets Prison Time." *Deseret News*, February 6.

Marquet International Ltd. (2011). *The Marquet Report on Ponzi Schemes*. Wellesley, MA.

Minutes, Sentencing Hearing. (2017). Utah v. Randall, No. 141906717. Third Judicial District, Salt Lake County, State of Utah. February 6.

OSC (Order to Show Cause). (2012). In the Matter of: Dee Allen Randall, et al. Division of Securities, Utah Department of Commerce, SD-12-0079-0085. Third Judicial District, Salt Lake County, Utah. December 18.

Plea Agreement (2016). Utah v. Randall, Case No. 141906717. Third Judicial District, Salt Lake County, Utah. Plea Agreement, Statement of Defendant in Support of Guilty Plea. July 11.

Protess, B. (2015). "Utah Passes White-Collar Felon Registry." *New York Times*, March 11.

Trustee's Final Report (2019). In re: Dee Allen Randall, et al., Bankruptcy Case No. 10-37546. U.S. Bankruptcy Court, D. Utah. Trustee's Final Report and Motion for Entry of Final Decree and for Order Closing Consolidated Case. January 18.

Utah Office of the Attorney General (2018). Stop Fraud Utah https://attorneygeneral.utah.gov/utfraud/. Updated June 18.

FOUR

Health Care Fraud

UNITED STATES V. ARMANDO GONZALEZ

THE HEALTH CARE INDUSTRY IS A MASSIVE part of the American economy, accounting for more than $3.6 trillion in expenditures in 2018 (Kamal and Cox, 2019). And because the government understands that where there is money, there is fraud, federal law enforcement agencies have dedicated resources to policing this industry for fraud and abuse. Health care fraud costs consumers and the government billions of dollars each year. Common fraud schemes in this industry include fraudulent billing for services, tests, prescriptions, and devices that aren't necessary or aren't actually provided; paying kickbacks to providers for referrals; and falsifying medical records to justify unnecessary treatment. These practices steal money from insurers, but they also drive up the cost of health care for everyone else. Health care fraud can lead to patient harm because it can include schemes to dilute medications or substitute counterfeit medical devices. It also includes the practices of unnecessary surgery and "ghost surgery"; in the latter case, a patient agrees to undergo surgery with an experienced surgeon, who then allows a doctor with far less experience to do the actual procedure.

The government agencies tasked with investigating and prosecuting health care fraud include the Office of Inspector General for the United States Department of Health and Human Services, the US Food and Drug Administration (FDA), the Drug Enforcement Administration (DEA), the Federal Bureau of Investigation (FBI), and the Internal Revenue Service (IRS), along with various state agencies, such as those that oversee Medicaid. The Medicare Fraud Strike Force is a joint initiative of those agencies that work with state and local partners to crack down on health care fraud that affects government-sponsored medical programs. Since 2007, nearly four

11th Circuit Court of Appeals

18 U.S.C. § 1347—Health Care Fraud

It's a Federal crime to knowingly and willfully execute, or attempt to execute, a scheme or artifice to defraud a health care benefit program, or to get any of the money or property owned by, or under the custody or control of, a health care benefit program by means of false or fraudulent pretenses, representations, or promises.

The Defendant can be found guilty of this offense only if all the following facts are proved beyond a reasonable doubt:

(1) the Defendant knowingly executed, or attempted to execute, a scheme or artifice to defraud a health-care benefit program, [or to obtain money or property owned by, or under the custody or control of, a health-care benefit program] by means of false or fraudulent pretenses, representations, or promises;

(2) the health care benefit program affected interstate commerce;

(3) the false or fraudulent pretenses, representations, or promises related to a material fact;

(4) the Defendant acted willfully and intended to defraud; and

(5) the Defendant did so in connection with the delivery of or payment for health-care benefits, items, or services.

. . .

A "scheme to defraud" includes any plan or course of action intended to deceive or cheat someone out of money or property by using false or fraudulent pretenses, representations, or promises relating to a material fact.

A statement or representation is "false" or "fraudulent" if it is about a material fact that the speaker knows is untrue or makes with reckless indifference as to the truth and makes with the intent to defraud. A statement or representation may be "false" or "fraudulent" when it's a half truth or effectively conceals a material fact and is made with the intent to defraud.

A "material fact" is an important fact that a reasonable person would use to decide whether to do or not do something. A fact is "material" if it has the capacity or natural tendency to influence a person's decision. It doesn't matter whether the decision-maker actually relied on the statement or knew or should have known that the statement was false.

To act with "intent to defraud" means to do something with the specific intent to deceive or cheat someone, usually for personal financial gain or to cause financial loss to someone else.

thousand defendants have been charged in cases led by the strike force (DOJ Los Angeles, 2019).

A number of federal criminal statutes specifically address health care fraud, and the government can also apply any number of general fraud and conspiracy criminal charges where appropriate. The following case illustrates how the federal government is attempting to coordinate its resources in order to tackle large-scale fraud schemes that siphon tens of millions of dollars from insurers and federal health care programs.

The case of *United States v. Armando Gonzalez, et al.* involved false claims, kickbacks for patient referrals, forged medical records, and some interesting non-health-care-related issues about pretrial detention. As you read about the investigation and prosecution of those involved in Healthcare Solutions Network, Inc., think about at what stage oversight and regulation could have caught this fraud scheme earlier or prevented it altogether. Are there new rules that could be put in place, or is this a matter of enforcing existing rules?

THE CRIME

Starting in the mid-2000s, Healthcare Solutions Network, Inc. (HCSN), operated three community mental health centers in Miami, Florida. Beginning in 2008, the company expanded, adding a facility in Hendersonville, North Carolina (Indictment, 2012). Community mental health care centers provide treatment for mentally ill patients, including those who suffer from schizophrenia or bipolar disease (42 CFR 485.904 et seq.). Medicare and Medicaid pay for patients to receive psychiatric care outside a hospital setting, an arrangement referred to as a partial hospitalization program, or PHP. The centers provide group and family counseling, occupational therapy, social workers, and diagnostic services, and administer drugs that patients cannot self-administer. They also offer intensive, all-day individual and group therapy, but are not allowed to offer activities that are simply recreational or diversionary. Mental health treatment has evolved and improved drastically in the past seventy-five years, with medication and therapy allowing many people diagnosed with mental health problems to live full and independent lives (Drake et al., 2003). PHP centers are designed to provide structured and intensive programs that enable patients to live on their own, keeping costs far lower than for a hospital stay. Doctors often refer patients to the centers as a way to avoid hospitalization, or following an in-patient stay for treatment of severe mental illness. Because the patient has to be able to participate and benefit from the counseling program, the Medicare-funded PHP does not cover patients with dementia, Alzheimer's disease, or other memory problems.

PHP facilities that seek reimbursement under this program must meet strict documentation requirements, starting at intake, when medical personnel document a patient's history, symptoms, medications, and other treatment notes. Patients are referred by a psychiatrist or mental health specialist and must be admitted under the supervision of a physician, with a written treatment plan addressing the patient's needs. Details of the patient's participation in therapeutic activities must be charted to show progress. Medicare requires justification for continued treatment in this program, consistent with the patient's medical needs. Typically, a patient stays in a PHP for two to three weeks, and longer enrollment periods tend to indicate that the treatment is not effective.

HCSN was a successful business enterprise, garnering $28 million in revenue from the Medicare program for seniors and the disabled over seven years. To review the care provided by Healthcare Solutions Network, the company paid an independent contractor, Psychiatric Consulting Network, Inc. (PCN), to monitor care and ensure that treatment was appropriate. Another company, Procare Management and Financial Network, Inc., handled the billing (Indictment, 2012).

When the North Carolina facility opened, other Hendersonville practitioners welcomed it to the community. The new center offered perks, such as transportation for patients in rural areas (Hoban, 2012). But despite the appearances, all was not as it seemed at the four HCSN centers. As a panel of appellate judges found in 2018, "From intake to discharge, HCSN organized its business around procuring, retaining, and readmitting patients to maximize billing potential, without respect to patients' health needs" (*United States v. Crabtree, et al.,* 878 F.3d 1274, 1279 [11th Cir. 2018]). Starting with recruitment, HCSN violated the law at every stage of the process. The company paid kickbacks in cash to assisted-living facilities and hospital employees in exchange for beneficiary information—even when the patients were not eligible for PHP treatment (Plea Agreement, 2012). That inconvenience was easily taken care of by altering patient records to conceal disqualifying symptoms or diagnoses, such as evidence that a person suffered from dementia. Patients were treated at the centers for unusually long periods of time, up to four months, then discharged and immediately admitted to another HCSN facility.

HCSN employees altered records, including patient notes and billing sheets, to justify Medicare claims and pass audits. "Therapists fabricated therapy notes for absent patients, falsified details from therapy sessions, and 'cloned' notes by copy and pasting therapy notes, verbatim, from one patient's file to another's. 'Ghost lists' of non-existent patients helped HCSN employees organize 'ghost billings' of services that never took place," the court noted (*Crabtree*, 878 F.3d at 1280). While the company billed government-sponsored health programs for therapy and treatment, patients spent their time at the center watching Disney movies, playing bingo, and having barbeques (DOJ Miami, 2013). Federal authorities estimated that, over seven years, from 2004 to 2011, the HCSN's owner, Armando Gonzalez, submitted approximately $63 million in fraudulent claims to Medicare and Medicaid programs.

The vast company-wide fraud scheme was organized by Gonzalez, who might have seemed an unlikely candidate to own and operate a small chain of mental health centers. Gonzalez was a convicted cocaine trafficker who had spent more than five years in prison after a 1984 conviction (Hoban, 2012).

THE INVESTIGATION AND PROSECUTION

On May 2, 2012, teams of agents swooped in and arrested Gonzalez and others who were alleged to have been involved in the Healthcare Solutions Network fraud scheme. But this was only one part of a joint effort to crack down on health care fraud that day. In all, more than two hundred agents, forensic examiners, and analysts from multiple agencies arrested 107 people as part of a massive sweep by the Medicare Fraud Strike Force. The arrests took place in seven cities, including Miami, Detroit, Houston, Tampa, and Los Angeles, and involved allegations of $452 million in false billing. Those arrested included doctors, nurses, and other licensed professionals, apprehended for their part in various schemes to defraud the health care programs (DOJ OPA, 2012). The investigations were largely data driven.

Gonzalez was arrested in North Carolina, though the federal case against him and other HCSN employees was filed in the US District Court for the Southern District of Florida. He was charged with one count of conspiracy to commit health care fraud (18 U.S.C. § 1347), three counts of conspiracy to receive and pay health care kickbacks (18 U.S.C. § 371), and thirteen separate counts of money laundering (18 U.S.C. §§ 1956(a)(1)(B)(i), 1956(h), and 1957).

To pull off such a complex fraud scheme required a large cast of coconspirators, and Gonzalez had many employees to help him. Among them was John T., a registered nurse who reviewed records and submitted HCSN claims. John was also president of Psychiatric Consulting Network, Inc., the purportedly independent contractor that reviewed HCSN claims for necessity and appropriateness (Indictment, 2012). Seven other employees were taking part in the conspiracies by falsifying records, paying kickbacks for referrals, submitting false claims, and otherwise assisting Gonzalez in the scheme. In 2013, seven additional employees who worked at an HCSN facility in Miami (HCSN-West) were indicted on similar charges in a separate indictment, including Dr. Roger Rousseau, a psychiatrist and the medical director of HCSN, and three state-licensed therapists (Weaver, 2014).

The government also sought forfeiture of property it could trace back to the illegally gained profits, including seventeen vehicles and two pieces of real estate in North Carolina. In all, the forfeiture allegation totaled more than $28 million, the amount the government said was the gross proceeds of the crime (Indictment, 2012).

While most defendants were released after posting bond, the government sought to keep Gonzalez in custody until his trial, arguing that he was a flight risk (Detention Order, 2012). Due to his criminal history, the government estimated that Gonzalez was facing a potential sentence of 30 years to life if he were convicted at trial. The prosecutors also argued that the $28 million in proceeds had disappeared. The lengthy prospective sentence, coupled with Gonzalez' access to substantial financial resources, met the legal burden to keep him in custody, according to the government.

A defendant can be detained pending trial if "no condition or combination of conditions will reasonably assure the appearance of the person as required and the safety of any other person and the community" (18 U.S.C. § 3142(e)(1)). The court must weigh four factors: (1) the nature and circumstances of the offenses charged; (2) the weight of the evidence against the defendant; (3) the history of the defendant whether the defendant has a history of failing to obey court orders; and (4) the nature and seriousness of the danger that the defendant's release would pose to any person or to the community (18 U.S.C. § 3142(g)(1)–(4)).

Gonzalez waived the detention hearing in North Carolina and was transported to Miami. Six weeks later, a magistrate granted Gonzalez' release on house arrest with a $300,000 bond that carried a Nebbia condition—a requirement that the person posting the bond disclose the source of the funds, to ensure that it is not the proceeds of criminal activity. The prosecutor objected and filed a motion to have a district court judge reconsider the bond.

On review, the court held that the government's case against Gonzalez was strong, with several codefendants pleading guilty and agreeing to cooperate against Gonzalez. The charges themselves were serious and carried a lengthy sentence should Gonzalez be convicted. The court also noted that the defendant was born in Cuba, and though he did not have any immediate family there and held no Cuban passport, "given the lengthy prison sentence Defendant faces and the uncontroverted fact that Cuba does not extradite Cuban nationals who flee to the island, the Defendant poses a serious risk of flight" (Detention Order, 2012, p. 4). In addition, the government asserted that two cooperating witnesses had disclosed that Gonzalez threatened to harm them, an allegation that the court found credible. Gonzalez was remanded to custody until trial.

Gonzalez elected not to go to trial. In December 2012, he pleaded guilty in a cooperation agreement with the government. He entered a guilty plea to one count of conspiracy to defraud a health care benefit program and to one count of money laundering for using the proceeds of the fraud to live a lavish lifestyle (Plea Agreement, 2012). In exchange for his testimony against his codefendants and other cooperation, the government agreed to recommend a lower sentence. Gonzalez admitted that he knowingly conspired with others to defraud Medicare and Medicaid and that he engaged in transactions to conceal the nature of the proceeds. He said that he set up Psychiatric Consulting Network, Inc., the supposed independent third-party that reviewed HCSN claims, as a shell company to hide HCSN profits. His plea agreement set out details of the fraud scheme that implicated those who had worked for him.

SENTENCING

At the time of Armando Gonzalez's sentencing in February 2013, all but one of the defendants in his case had pleaded guilty. As a cooperating witness, Gonzalez could be called as a witness in the remaining defendant's trial. Because he had not yet testified, the government did not recommend a reduced sentence. The advisory sentencing range as calculated under the United States Sentencing Guidelines was 135 to 168 months, with both the prosecutor and defense asking for a low-end sentence of 135 months, or more than 11 years, in prison (Transcript, Sentencing Hearing, 2013). Judge Cecilia M. Altonaga instead sentenced Gonzalez to 14 years in prison, at the high end of the sentencing range. She described the factors explaining her decision: "Seven years, over $28 million stolen from the Federal Government's Medicare program in two states involving numerous participants. Brazen, calculated, committed by a man whose background and age are similar to my own, coming from the same community, aware of what the issues are here in South Florida, taking those issues to North Carolina in full and complete disregard of the crisis that we face as a nation, as a people, in keeping the Medicare program alive to give medical care to those who desperately need it, all for enriching himself" (Transcript, Sentencing Hearing, 2013, pp. 8–9). The serious nature of the offense called for a lengthy sentence, she said, and only such a significant sentence would deter others from committing this type of fraud. Gonzalez was also ordered to pay $28 million in restitution. He forfeited $1 million in various bank accounts, vehicles, and a home on one acre in North Carolina (Weaver, 2014).

Gonzalez testified at the trial of several HCSN therapists, resulting in convictions, including for Dr. Roger Rousseau, a psychiatrist for HCSN, who was later sentenced to 16 years in prison for his role in HCSN's fraud scheme. In addition, the government credited Gonzalez for extensive cooperation in directing investigators to additional participants in the scheme, including a hospital employee who received kickbacks in the parking lot (Transcript, Resentencing Hearing, 2015). Gonzalez also turned over HCSN business records, including patient files and census reports, that were used to prosecute other defendants.

For his cooperation, the government asked the court to revisit Gonzalez's sentence and reduce it by 37 percent to 106 months. At the resentencing hearing in 2015, Gonzalez's lawyer asked for a greater reduction, citing his extensive cooperation and stressing that it was a "painful" decision to testify against Dr. Rousseau, the longtime medical director of HCSN. The judge granted a reduction, but to 121 months.

TRENDS IN HEALTH CARE FRAUD

Since the high-profile arrest and conviction of Gonzalez and his coconspirators, as well as the many others arrested and charged in the 2012 task force

September 2019

Twenty-five people were charged in a Southern California sweep that targeted schemes involving false billings to Medicare, Medicaid, and other health plans for unnecessary or nonexistent services, testing, and prescriptions. Fourteen of the defendants charged in Los Angeles and Santa Ana were medical professionals, including doctors.

April 2019

Federal law enforcement arrested twenty-four people for allegedly running a $1.2 billion Medicare scheme that targeted elderly and disabled patients. Those arrested included owners of durable medical equipment companies whom the government accused of giving kickbacks and bribes to doctors to prescribe unnecessary medical devices, such as back, shoulder, knee, and wrist braces. Eight criminal cases were filed in seven U.S. district courts.

June 2018

More than 601 defendants were charged in a massive nationwide sweep by the Medicare Fraud Strike Force, including 165 doctors, nurses, and other licensed professionals, for allegedly participating in fraud schemes that generated $2 billion in false billings. The allegations ranged from illegal distribution of opioids to fraudulent billing for durable medical goods, such as orthopedic braces. The cases were filed in fifty-eight federal district courts.

sweep, the FBI and other agencies have continued to focus on fraud in the health care industry. The Medicare Fraud Strike Force, which coordinates federal, state, and local agencies in combatting fraud, has arrested nearly four thousand defendants, collectively responsible for $14 billion in false Medicare billings (DOJ Los Angeles, 2019). Fifteen strike forces operate in twenty-four federal districts.

But if even 3 percent of the annual health care expenditures are fraudulent, as estimated by the National Health Care Anti-fraud Association, that amounts to an estimated $68 billion a year—a huge industry in itself. The

Statutes commonly charged in federal health care criminal cases include:

- 18 U.S.C. § 1343 (wire fraud)
- 18 U.S.C. § 1347 (health care fraud)
- 18 U.S.C. § 1349 and 18 U.S.C. § 371 (attempt or conspiracy to commit health care fraud, and conspiracy to defraud the United States)
- 18 U.S.C. §§ 1956, 1957 (money laundering)
- 42 U.S.C. § 1320a-7b(b) (health care kickbacks)
- 18 U.S.C. §§ 1518, 1519 (obstruction)
- 18 U.S.C. § 669 (theft or embezzlement in connection with health care)
- 42 U.S.C. § 1320d-6 (unlawful use of health information)
- 18 U.S.C. § 1028A (aggravated identity theft)
- 18 U.S.C. § 1028(a)(7) (use of identification information)
- 18 U.S.C. § 1035 (false statements relating to health care matters)

sheer size and complexity of the health care system is the largest hurdle in antifraud efforts (NWCCC, 2013). In addition to federal health care programs, states can administer, regulate, and police their own programs. And it's difficult for all of these programs, as well as private insurers, to share information.

Some efforts to curb fraud have been enacted, particularly in the Patient Protection and Affordable Care Act (ACA), which included tougher screening for providers and suppliers who apply to participate in Medicare, Medicaid, and the Children's Health Insurance Program (CHIP). The ACA also authorized the suspension of Medicare payments to providers or suppliers who are under investigation for fraud. And the law increased federal sentencing guidelines for health care fraud, and added penalties for obstruction of an investigation or audit. In addition, the Center for Medicare and Medicaid Services has implemented new technologies that use advanced predictive modeling to fight fraud (NWCCC, 2013).

REFERENCES

Centers for Medicare & Medicaid Services, 42 CFR [Code of Federal Regulations] 485.904 et seq. Subpart J—Conditions of Participation: Community Mental Health Centers.

DOJ Los Angeles (Department of Justice, US Attorney's Office, Central District of California). (2018). "As Part of National Healthcare Fraud Sweep, Los Angeles–Based Prosecutors Filed 16 Cases Alleging $660 Million in Fraudulent Bills." United States Department of Justice. June 28. https://www.justice.gov/usao-cdca/pr/part-national-healthcare-fraud-sweep-los-angeles-based-prosecutors-filed-16-cases.

DOJ Miami (Department of Justice, US Attorney's Office, Southern District of Florida). (2013). "Supervisor of $63 Million Health Care Fraud Scheme Convicted." United States Department of Justice. April 25. https://www.justice.gov/usao-sdfl/pr/supervisor-63-million-health-care-fraud-scheme-convicted.

DOJ OPA (Department of Justice, Office of Public Affairs). (2012). "Medicare Fraud Strike Force Charges 107 Individuals for Approximately $452 Million in False Billing." United States Department of Justice. May 2. https://www.justice.gov/opa/pr/medicare-fraud-strike-force-charges-107-individuals-approximately-452-million-false-billing.

Drake, R., A. Green, K. Mueser, and H. Goldman (2003). "The History of Community Mental Health Treatment and Rehabilitation for Persons with Severe Mental Illness." *Community Mental Health Journal* 39, no. 5 (October).

Hoban, R. (2012). "Hendersonville Mental Health Provider Caught in Federal Medicare Fraud Sting." *North Carolina Health News,* May 4. https://www.northcarolinahealthnews.org/2012/05/04/hendersonville-mental-health-provider-caught-in-federal-medicare-fraud-sting/.

Kamal, R., and C. Cox (2019). "How Has U.S. Spending on Healthcare Changed over Time?" Peterson–Kaiser Family Foundation Health System Tracker. December 20. https://www.healthsystemtracker.org/chart-collection/u-s-spending-healthcare-changed-time/.

NWCCC (National White Collar Crime Center). (2013). "Health Care Fraud." Richmond, VA: NW3C.

Weaver, J. (2012). "Feds Fear Local Medicare Fraud Suspect Could Flee." BlueRidgeNow.com, May 7. https://www.blueridgenow.com/news/20120507/feds-fear-local-medicare-fraud-suspect-could-flee.

COURT DOCUMENTS

Detention Order. (2012). United States v. Gonzalez, et al., 12-cr-20291. S. Dist. Florida. July 6.

Indictment. (2012). United States v. Gonzalez, et al., 12-cr-20291. S. Dist. Florida. April 27.

Plea Agreement. (2012). United States v. Gonzalez, et al., 12-cr-20291. S. Dist. Florida. December 17.

Transcript, Resentencing Hearing. (2015). United States v. Gonzalez, et al., 12-cr-20291. S. Dist. Florida. October 9.

Transcript, Sentencing Hearing. (2013). United States v. Gonzalez, et al., 12-cr-20291. S. Dist. Florida. February 25.

United States v. Crabtree, 878 F.3d 1274 (11th Cir. 2018).

United States v. Ruiz, 698 Fed.Appx. 978 (11th Cir. 2017).

FIVE

Cybercrime

UNITED STATES V. ROMAN SELEZNEV

EVERY WEEK, IT SEEMS, A NEW WARNING goes out to consumers: a major corporation or financial institution has been hacked, and your data may have been exposed. These breaches can reveal sensitive information, including names, Social Security numbers, passwords, credit card and account numbers—data valuable to an underground network that packages it for sale to a criminal end user. In an online marketplace where buyers and sellers operate anonymously, it is often a challenge to pin an online breach to a real-life individual. Combating, investigating, and prosecuting these types of crimes can be further complicated if the perpetrators are outside the United States.

This chapter examines the case of *United States v. Roman Seleznev,* one of the largest cybercrime prosecutions. The case involves the hacking of point-of-sale systems used by small businesses to take credit card payments, the packaging and reselling of that credit card information, and a worldwide hunt for the perpetrator. It's also a rare success story of a large-scale cybercriminal being brought to the United States to stand trial. As you read this chapter, think about the international cooperation that was necessary to investigate and prosecute this case, and at what points the lack of cooperation with other jurisdictions hindered the case. Another interesting aspect of this case is attribution: how prosecutors prove that a certain individual is the person who is responsible for anonymous online activities.

THE CRIME

Investigators in the Pacific Northwest got their first introduction to this global cybercrime investigation through a report from a Schlotsky's Deli in

Coeur d'Alene, Idaho. In 2010, the store's owner reported a problem with its point-of-sale system, suspecting it had been targeted by cybercriminals. A Seattle police detective, David Dunn, who was a member of the Secret Service Electronic Crimes Task Force, responded and found that the system was beaming data out to servers in Russia. Soon, the investigation expanded to other restaurants in Washington State—bakeries, restaurants, pizza parlors. In each case, the point-of-sale system contained malicious software that located stored credit card numbers and then sent data overseas. The software appeared to have been installed by an intruder who had scanned the internet for open "ports" that allowed off-site tech support to remotely access a business's computer system for maintenance (Government's Trial Brief, 6).

The credit card information was sent back to collection servers where it was then sorted to determine the value of the data, such as credit card numbers, bank identification numbers, names of account holders, and personal identification numbers (PINs). From there, the data were posted for sale on websites known as "dump shops" and marketed to an underground network of buyers (Second Superseding Indictment, 2014).

These sites were already known to federal investigators. As early as 2005, the US Secret Service sought to identify the individual suspect whose online handle was "nCuX," a major player on forums where "carders" bought and sold stolen credit card data. "Carding" is the practice of hacking, stealing, and trafficking credit card data (Government's Trial Brief, 2016). Carding forums are marketplaces where carders, hidden behind online aliases, can sell the stolen credit information to users who then make fraudulent purchases. By 2009, investigators were fairly confident that the person going by "nCuX" was Roman Seleznev of Vladivostok, Russia. Federal agents attempted to gain international assistance and met with their Russian counterparts to share what they knew about the suspect and ask for help in apprehending him. This strategy backfired. Within a month, nCuX announced his retirement and disappeared from the internet (Black Hat USA, 2017). Investigators later learned that Seleznev's father was a member of the Russian parliament.

The investigation started over. But almost immediately a new online handle, "2Pac," appeared in the online carding forums, and the cybercrimes team suspected that it was the same person. Several new "dump shop" websites, including "Track2" and "Bulba," began trafficking in the same stolen credit card data. The sites even offered a service that would allowed buyers to check that the credit card accounts were still active and a guarantee to replace card numbers that were invalid (Second Superseding Indictment, 2014, p. 8). One site offered step-by-step tutorials on how to buy and use stolen credit card information for profit, even warning users "Remember this is Illegal way!" (Government's Sentencing Memorandum, 2017).

While investigating the 2010 breaches in the Pacific Northwest, the agents mapped the route the stolen data took and tracked it to the Track2 and Bulba sites, where the credit card numbers were offered for sale (Government's Trial Brief, 2016). Detective Dunn and Special Agent Keith Wojcieszek, a Washington, DC–based Secret Service agent, identified the infrastructure that Track2 used—including servers and email accounts. Most of the collection servers that aggregated the stolen credit card data were overseas, but a few were in Virginia and therefore subject to US jurisdiction. Dunn and Wojcieszek obtained search warrants to look for information that would lead to the identity of the site's operator. One server, known as HopOne, had collected hundreds of thousands of credit card numbers, including the ones in Washington State.

That server also contained a trail of electronic crumbs that led to the intruder. A forensic analysis found remnants of web-browsing history that included travel reservations for Roman Seleznev, including his date of birth, passport number, and the names of his wife, daughter, other family members, and two associates (Government's Trial Brief, 2016). It also revealed two email accounts that gave the agents a new direction in which to search. Search warrants for the email accounts led to billing statements for other servers, and email traffic confirmed the registration of another site thought to be linked to Seleznev.

One of those email accounts was particularly revealing, producing evidence such as emails to Seleznev from his wife in which she attached pictures of herself and their daughter; other emails addressed to Roman Seleznev; receipts for flower deliveries to Seleznev's wife at their home address; and an invoice addressed to Roman Seleznev that listed a phone number he was known to use. The emails also revealed usernames and passwords commonly used by Seleznev, further linking him to the intrusion (Government's Trial Brief, 2016, p. 9). Investigators found a particular Yahoo email address used to register the Track2 website, and obtained a search warrant for that email account. While that search turned up no evidence linked to Seleznev, investigators learned that the account used the username "smaus" and password "ochko."

Now that investigators had a name to link to the crime, they could go after their suspect. A sealed indictment was filed in March 2011 charging Seleznev with six counts of bank fraud (18 U.S.C. § 1344), eight counts of intentional damage to a protected computer (18 U.S.C. § 1030(a)(5)(A)), eight counts of obtaining information from a protected computer (18 U.S.C. § 1030(a)(2)), one violation of possessing fifteen or more unauthorized access devices (18 U.S.C. § 1029(a)(3)), two charges of trafficking in unauthorized access devices (18 U.S.C. § 1029(a)(2)), and five counts of aggravated identity theft (18 U.S.C. 1028A(c)). They had an arrest warrant, but Roman Seleznev avoided US jurisdiction. Investigators began stalking him around the globe.

A month after the sealed indictment was filed, Seleznev was severely injured in a terrorist bombing at a restaurant in Morocco (Black Hat USA, 2017). Suffering major head trauma and other wounds, he was airlifted back to Moscow, where he remained in a coma for several weeks and was hospitalized for months. In the meantime, his online business slowed, and his associates asked customers of Track2 and Bulba to be patient while the boss recovered.

Seleznev and his business did eventually bounce back, and the US agents continued to watch for him, but he continued to carefully avoid U.S. jurisdiction. On July 1, 2014, agents learned that he was vacationing in the Maldives, a small chain of islands in the Indian Ocean. The information set off a flurry of activity for those involved in the case (Government's Sentencing Memorandum, 2017, p. 11).

The agents had four days to (1) seek internal US government clearances to conduct a foreign operation; (2) obtain agreement from the Maldives to turn Seleznev over without a formal extradition treaty; (3) mobilize Secret Service agents to the Maldives (an eighteen-hour flight from Hawaii); (4) coordinate the logistics of the apprehension with the local authorities; (5) arrange for private transportation (that is, a private jet with sufficient range to fly many thousands of miles over water) to take Seleznev to the nearest US territory; and (6) take custody of Seleznev.

The United States does not have an extradition treaty with the Maldives, but US officials convinced the authorities there to expel Seleznev from the country to US custody (Black Hat USA, 2017). He was arrested at the airport on July 5, 2014, and taken to Guam, where he had an initial appearance in a US federal court. He pleaded not guilty to all charges.

Seleznev, thirty years old, had genuine health concerns stemming from the 2011 bombing in Morocco, which had left him with a significant head injury. He fought extradition to the United States, claiming he'd been "kidnapped" in violation of international law, and enlisted the Russian government's assistance. He lost that battle, however, and was transported to Seattle to stand trial.

Roman Seleznev was arraigned in a federal court in Guam on August 8, 2014. He entered a not guilty plea to all charges. Once transported to Seattle, a judge ordered his detention pending trial, finding that Seleznev posed a flight risk (Carter, 2014).

In the following two years before the trial began in August 2016, Roman Seleznev hired and fired numerous attorneys and, prosecutors alleged, discussed how to bribe the prosecutors to make the trial go away (Black Hat USA, 2017). Seleznev also asked to represent himself at the pretrial motions stage of the proceedings and filed several motions to dismiss that alleged prosecutorial misconduct. His motions were denied. He also filed a motion to suppress the evidence found on his laptop, claiming that the government had tampered with it. The court found no evidence that the computer had been altered.

EVIDENCE AT TRIAL

When Roman Seleznev was arrested in the Maldives, authorities seized his laptop and phone, both of which provided a wealth of new evidence against him (Black Hat USA, 2017). The laptop contained 250 "dump files" that held 1.7 million stolen credit card numbers; pictures and text used to create one of the dump sites; and chat logs between 2Pac and other carders in which they discussed buying and selling credit card data (Government's Trial Brief, 2016). Another key piece of evidence that linked Seleznev to the servers was an electronic password "cheat sheet" that listed his usernames and passwords, including frequent use of "smaus" as a username and "ochko" as a password. This was the same combination as the Yahoo email account used to create the Track2 and Bulba sites.

Two other items on the laptop caught investigators' attention. First, chat logs from 2008 in which Seleznev bragged to an associate that he had protection through law enforcement contacts in the computer crime squad of the FSB, the Russian federal security service. In 2010, he told someone else that the FSB knew who he was and was working with the FBI (Government's Sentencing Memorandum, 2017). This explained how Seleznev learned about the Secret Service's 2009 attempt to get Russian law enforcement's assistance to arrest him. The second item of interest was evidence that prior to traveling,

Seleznev had searched federal court records for an indictment in his name and his online aliases, using the online court filing system PACER (Government's Sentencing Memorandum, 2017).

On the stand during more than two days of testimony, Detective David Dunn walked through all of the electronic links between the computer breaches, the online sales of stolen credit card information, and Roman Seleznev. Building the case at trial is a challenge, observed Norman Barbosa, one of the two assistant US attorneys involved in the Seleznev case, "because attribution is everything. There's no debate that a crime occurred. It's not a fraud case where you're arguing about whether a security was fraudulent. This definitely happened. It was definitely illegal. The question is purely, who did it. And you're dealing with the anonymity of the internet, where it's all done with false names" (personal communication, September 23, 2019).

During the nine-day jury trial held in Seattle, business owners testified about the money they had to spend to install new computers after their point-of-sale systems were compromised by hackers—a huge expense for a small business operating on slim margins (Bellisle, 2016). The owner of Seattle's Broadway Grill testified that the breach instantly cut his revenue by 40 percent, eventually sending the business into bankruptcy (Government's Sentencing Memorandum, 2017). Another restaurant owner said he had a "nervous breakdown" due to the effect on his business. Another said that six years later, he was still trying to pay down the debt he took on to address the intrusion.

Prosecutors alleged that Seleznev's scheme enabled $170 million in fraudulent credit card purchases and was linked to thirty-seven hundred banks around the world. Not all of the hundreds of businesses harmed by the hacking testified at trial, but many later submitted victim-impact statements and claims for damages that provided examples of how they were affected. The Houston Zoo reported that it had put off planned upgrades to facilities that would have "benefitted its millions of guests, improved the work environment of its staff, and enhanced the lives of its animals" (Government's Sentencing Memorandum, 2017, p. 10). The owner of a market in New Jersey spent thousands of dollars in response to the hack and said that the business still hadn't recovered.

Seleznev's defense aimed at the sufficiency of the government's case, arguing that there was reasonable doubt about whether the anonymous online acts were committed by this one individual.

On August 25, 2016, the jury returned guilty verdicts on thirty-eight of the forty criminal counts. Seleznev was acquitted on one count of intentional

9th Circuit Court of Appeals

18 U.S.C. § 1029(a)(2). Unauthorized Access Devices—Using or Trafficking.

The defendant is charged in [Count ___ of] the indictment with trafficking in unauthorized access devices during a period of one year in violation of Section 1029(a)(2) of Title 18 of the United States Code.

In order for the defendant to be found guilty of that charge, the government must prove each of the following elements beyond a reasonable doubt:

First, the defendant knowingly [used] [trafficked in] the unauthorized access devices at any time during a one-year period [beginning [date], and ending [date]];

Second, by [using] [trafficking in] the unauthorized access devices during that period, the defendant obtained [anything of value worth $1,000 or more] during that period;

Third, the defendant acted with the intent to defraud; and

Fourth, the defendant's conduct in some way affected commerce between one state and another state, or between a state of the United States and a foreign country.

An "unauthorized access device" is any access device that is lost, stolen, expired, revoked, canceled, or obtained with intent to defraud.

To "traffic" in an access device means to transfer or otherwise dispose of it to another, or to obtain control of it with intent to transfer or dispose of it.

18 U.S.C. § 1029(a)(3). Access Devices—Unlawfully Possessing Fifteen or More

The defendant is charged in [Count ___ of] the indictment with unlawful possession of access devices in violation of Section 1029(a)(1) of Title 18 of the United States Code.

In order for the defendant to be found guilty of that charge, the government must prove each of the following elements beyond a reasonable doubt:

First, the defendant knowingly possessed at least fifteen unauthorized access devices at the same time;

Second, the defendant knew that the devices were unauthorized;

Third, the defendant acted with the intent to defraud; and

Fourth, the defendant's conduct in some way affected commerce between one state and another state, or between a state of the United States and a foreign country.

An "unauthorized access device" is any access device that is lost, stolen, expired, revoked, canceled, or obtained with intent to defraud.

18 U.S.C. § 1029. Access Device—Defined.

An "access device" means any card, plate, code, account number, electronic serial number, mobile identification number, personal identification number, or other telecommunications service, equipment, or instrument identifier, or other means of account access, that can be used alone or in conjunction with another access device, to obtain money, goods, services, or any other thing of value, or that can be used to initiate a transfer of funds (other than a transfer originated solely by paper instrument).

18 U.S.C. § 1030(a)(5)(A). Intentional Damage to a Protected Computer.

The defendant is charged in [Count ___ of] the indictment with transmitting [a program] [a code] [a command] [information] to a computer [system], intending to cause damage, in violation of Section 1030(a)(5) of Title 18 of the United States Code.

In order for the defendant to be found guilty of that charge, the government must prove each of the following elements beyond a reasonable doubt:

First, the defendant knowingly caused the transmission of [a program] [a code] [a command] [information] to a computer without authorization;

Second, as a result of the transmission, the defendant intentionally impaired the [integrity] [availability] of [data] [a program] [a system] [information]; and

Third, the computer was [exclusively for the use of a financial institution or the United States government] [used in or affected interstate or foreign commerce or communication] [located outside the United States but was used in a manner that affects interstate or foreign commerce or communication of the United States] [not exclusively for the use of a financial institution or the United States government, but the defendant's transmission affected the computer's use by or for a financial institution or the United States government].

damage to a protected computer and another count of wire fraud, both relating to an alleged computer intrusion at the same pizzeria.

SENTENCING

Seleznev returned to court for sentencing on April 21, 2017. As often happens, the two parties had very different views of how a proper sentence should be determined. Depending on who was talking about him, Roman Seleznev was either the privileged son of a member of the Russian parliament or a young man who was abandoned by his father, lost his mother at a young age, and grew up poor and alone (Carter, 2016; Personal Statement by Roman Seleznev, 2017).

Seleznev's attorney painted him as a man who had made terrible choices in the past, but who wanted now to cooperate with law enforcement and was on a better path (Transcript, Sentencing Hearing, 2017). Seleznev submitted a handwritten letter to the judge that explained his history and attempted to correct the impression that he'd benefited from his father's political connections. In fact, he said, nothing could be further from the truth. Seleznev said his father abandoned his family, leaving him and his mother with little to live on (Defendant's Sentencing Memorandum, 2017). He acknowledged his criminal activity, but said it was the only option he thought he had to support himself as a young man without resources or education. He also asked the judge to consider his ongoing health issues from the bombing, including severe seizures that required medication.

The government's sentencing memorandum took a different view of Seleznev. He had lived large and owned two properties in Bali, Indonesia, and spent his time jetting between Bali and Vladivostok, Russia. He stayed in luxury hotels, and spent $20,000 at the resort in the Maldives prior to his arrest. The government estimated that through a single payment service, Liberty Reserve, he took in $17 million between 2010 and 2013. Liberty Reserve was seized by the government in 2014 in connection with a separate criminal investigation, and Seleznev's account was found in the company's records (see chapter 7, "Money Laundering"). But prosecutors did not know how much Seleznev had profited from the scheme, because he used Bitcoin, WebMoney, and other payment systems that ensure anonymity.

The first step in determining a sentence in federal court is to calculate an advisory sentencing range under the United States Sentencing Guidelines (USSG). The guidelines seek to quantify all aspects of the crime and the defendant's role in it and to promote consistent resolutions throughout the federal court system. Cases relating to financial crimes fall under Section 2B1.1 of the Guidelines, and determining the sentence is largely driven by the amount of money lost due to the fraudulent behavior. In Seleznev's case, the victims of the computer intrusions lost $170 million, prosecutors estimated. But for purposes of sentencing, the Guidelines calculate loss based on how many credit cards Seleznev stole, possessed, or used (USSG § 2B1.1, App. Note 4(F)). Each card is valued at a minimum of $500. Though Seleznev had 1.7 million credit card numbers on his laptop when he was arrested, the evidence at trial proved that he stole 2.4 million credit cards over several years. That brought the loss amount for sentencing purposes to $1.2 billion.

There are additional specific offense characteristics that the court also must take into account. Aggravating factors include how many victims were involved, whether the defendant was in the business of receiving stolen property, whether the fraudulent scheme was committed from outside the United States, and whether the criminal conduct involved sophisticated means. The court found that all of these aggravating factors applied in Seleznev's case.

In addition to specific offense characteristics that the court uses to tally a score based on the criminal conduct, the court must also look at the defendant's specific conduct relating to any crime, such as the defendant's role in the offense. Here, the prosecutors argued that Seleznev was a leader of the operation. The court declined to adopt that finding, as it was unclear who else was involved in Seleznev's enterprise.

Under the Sentencing Guidelines, Seleznev's advisory sentence was life imprisonment. But calculating the advisory sentencing range is only the starting point. The sentence must be calculated based on all of the factors set forth in 18 U.S.C. § 3553(a).

The government was not seeking a life sentence for Seleznev, though it noted that this was an unprecedented prosecution and the sentence needed to have a strong deterrent value (Government's Sentencing Memorandum, 2017). Rather, government prosecutors sought a sentence of 30 years, plus restitution of nearly $170 million. This sentence was similar to that recommended by the United States Probation Department's in its pre-sentence report: a total term of imprisonment of 27 years and nearly $170 million in restitution to the identified victims (Defendant's Sentencing Memorandum, 2017).

Seleznev's attorneys urged the court to depart downward from probation's recommendation, for several reasons. Seleznev argued that the calculated loss of about $1.2 billion substantially overstated the actual loss of $170 million attributed to the defendant. And the attorneys argued that sentencing Seleznev to decades in prison went against the parsimony clause in the sentencing law, which directs the court to impose a punishment that is "sufficient, but not greater than necessary," to achieve the goals of the sentencing law (18 U.S.C. § 3553(a)). Due to his health issues, a lengthy sentence would be even harsher for Seleznev than others, his lawyer said. As he was not a citizen, once Seleznev was released from prison, he would be deported back to Russia.

Finally, Seleznev was sorry for his actions, his attorney said. He was embarrassed and humiliated by his conduct, and he deeply regretted the loss to the many victims (Defendant's Sentencing Memorandum, 2017, p. 15). At the sentencing hearing, in his allocution (the opportunity to speak to the court), Seleznev again apologize for his conduct. He told the court that "not one day has passed which I have not felt extreme sympathy and sadness for the crimes I commit and negative impact to my victims" (Transcript, Sentencing Hearing, 2017, p. 37). Seleznev said he was ashamed of his conduct, did not want to minimize the seriousness of his crime, and understood that a long sentence would likely be imposed. He stressed that he missed his family in Russia and wished to get back to them as soon as possible.

US district court judge Richard A. Jones recognized the lack of parental guidance that Seleznev had had as a child. But on the whole, the judge believed, Seleznev's life demonstrated far more aggravating circumstances then mitigating ones. Most of his adult life had been dedicated to credit card fraud. And while Seleznev had apologized to the court for his conduct and expressed remorse, the court found no true acceptance of responsibility for his conduct. Judge Jones noted that Seleznev had had multiple opportunities in his life to reset his "moral navigation system and avoid a life of crime" (Transcript, Sentencing Hearing, 2017, p. 44). The sentence that Seleznev and his attorney sought, essentially asking for time served or probation, would have no deterrent value, one of the factors the court must consider under 18 U.S.C. § 3553(a). In the end, the court imposed a 27-year sentence, following the recommendation of the probation office. The breakdown of the sentence was 300 months on most of the charges, concurrent with one another and concurrent with other counts. Under the statute, counts 39 and 40, the identity theft convictions, carry mandatory consecutive sentences of 24 months each.

Roman Seleznev was ordered to serve 27 years in prison and pay nearly $170 million to his many victims. He was also charged and convicted in two other federal cases. In the US district court in Nevada, Seleznev was charged for his role in a $50 million scheme to traffic in stolen credit cards and counterfeit and stolen identities (DOJ OPA, 2017). Seleznev pleaded guilty in the Nevada case to one count of participation in a racketeering enterprise, admitting to selling stolen credit card accounts for approximately $20 each.

He also pleaded guilty to one count of conspiracy to commit bank fraud in a case filed in Georgia, where he admitted that he acted as a "casher" in a 2008 scheme in which hackers infiltrated a company's computer systems and accessed 45.5 million debit card numbers that they used to withdraw more than $9.4 million in cash from 2,100 ATMs in 280 cities around the world over a twelve-hour period. In each case, Seleznev was sentenced to 168 months, to run concurrently with the sentence imposed in the Washington case.

In all of these cases, the victims were unlikely to recover any money. Norman Barbosa, the former assistant US attorney who prosecuted the Washington case, says that Seleznev's money was in Russian banks and remained out of reach of US authorities. Seleznev also kept some profits in Bitcoin, but the government did not recover Seleznev's wallet. Even with a court order, it is difficult to recover money from overseas jurisdictions.

THE FUTURE OF CYBERCRIME

At the time of Seleznev's trial in 2016, his was the largest hacking case prosecuted by the federal government. Since then, several other defendants in large-scale cybercrime cases have been extradited to the United States to stand trial, but many are beyond the reach of US law enforcement—particularly those in Russia, Barbosa noted. "There's a huge problem of impunity for Russian hackers, the difficulty in bringing anyone to justice," he said. The Secret Service agents attempted to work with Russian law enforcement, only to have them tip off Seleznev (Government's Sentencing Memorandum, 2017).

"One big trend over the last five years is that there is more nation-state involvement in computer crimes, hacking more for political purposes and espionage," Barbosa said.

18 U.S.C. § 3553(a). Imposition of a Sentence.

(a) Factors to Be Considered in Imposing a Sentence. The court shall impose a sentence sufficient, but not greater than necessary, to comply with the purposes set forth in paragraph (2) of this subsection. The court, in determining the particular sentence to be imposed, shall consider—

(1) the nature and circumstances of the offense and the history and characteristics of the defendant;

(2) the need for the sentence imposed—
    (A) to reflect the seriousness of the offense, to promote respect for the law, and to provide just punishment for the offense;
    (B) to afford adequate deterrence to criminal conduct;
    (C) to protect the public from further crimes of the defendant; and
    (D) to provide the defendant with needed educational or vocational training, medical care, or other correctional treatment in the most effective manner;

(3) the kinds of sentences available;

(4) the kinds of sentence and the sentencing range established for—
    (A) the applicable category of offense committed by the applicable category of defendant as set forth in the [United States Sentencing Guidelines] . . .

(5) any pertinent policy statement—
    (A) issued by the Sentencing Commission . . .

(6) the need to avoid unwarranted sentence disparities among defendants with similar records who have been found guilty of similar conduct; and

(7) the need to provide restitution to any victims of the offense.

Cybercriminals are becoming more sophisticated and organized. As technology evolves, it has become easier for hackers and carders to cover their tracks through encryption or by conducting business on the Dark Web, websites that use anonymity tools to hide their IP addresses. The typical carder is also becoming better organized, operating as a criminal enterprise with multiple layers of actors running the operation as if it were a business, Barbosa reported. These suspects, he said, "are far more organized than Seleznev."

Despite the challenges, according to Barbosa, these cases are solved using the same investigative techniques and dogged detective work as with any other crime.

"Any online investigation involves tracing every lead and looking for a mistake. You'll follow a hundred leads to find one mistake," he said; in Seleznev's case, he used one of his carder email accounts to order flowers for his wife. The key is perseverance in following every lead. "What was striking about the investigation [is] that it was just good detective work and attention to detail that picked it apart," Barbosa observed. "Even though it's online, you're doing the same things that detectives do in traditional cases—going to the crime scene and looking for anything that can be evidence of a crime."

Seleznev appealed his conviction and sentence to the Ninth Circuit US Court of Appeals, which affirmed his conviction in April 2019. Upon his release, scheduled for early 2038, Seleznev will be deported to Russia.

REFERENCES

Bellisle, M. (2016). "Trial of Alleged Russian Master Hacker Begins This Week; Targets Were Credit Cards Used at Pizza Places." *Seattle Times,* August 14.

Black Hat USA. (2017). "Ochko123—How the Feds Caught Russian Mega Carder Roman Seleznev." YouTube, updated August 25. https://www.youtube.com/watch?v=6Chp12sEnWk&feature=youtu.be.

Carter, M. (2014). "Accused Russian Hacker Must Stay in Custody, Judge Says." *Seattle Times,* August 15.

Carter, M. (2016). "Feds Outline Case against Alleged Russian Hacker." *Seattle Times,* August 15.

DOJ OPA (Department of Justice, Office of Public Affairs). (2017). "Russian Cyber-criminal Sentenced to 14 Years in Prison for Role in Organized Cybercrime Ring Responsible for $50 Million in Online Identity Theft and $9 Million Bank Fraud Conspiracy." United States Department of Justice. November 30. https://www.justice.gov/opa/pr/russian-cyber-criminal-sentenced-14-years-prison-role-organized-cybercrime-ring-responsible.

COURT DOCUMENTS

Defendant's Sentencing Memorandum. (2017). United States v. Seleznev, 11-cr-0070. W. Dist. Washington. April 14.

Government's Sentencing Memorandum. (2017). United States v. Seleznev, 11-cr-0070. W. Dist. Washington. April 14.

Government's Trial Brief. (2016). United States v. Seleznev, 11-cr-0070. W. Dist. Washington. July 25.

Indictment. (2012). United States v. Seleznev, 11-cr-0070. W. Dist. Washington. March 3.

Personal Statement by Roman Seleznev. (2017). United States v. Seleznev, 11-cr-0070. W. Dist. Washington. April 10.

Second Superseding Indictment. (2014). United States v. Seleznev, 11-cr-0070. W. Dist. Washington. October 8.

Transcript, Sentencing Hearing. (2017). United States v. Seleznev, 11-cr-0070. W. Dist. Washington. April 21.

United States v. Seleznev, 766 Fed.Appx. 531 (9th Cir. 2019).

SIX

Corporate Criminal Liability

UNITED STATES V. GENERAL MOTORS

THIS CASE STUDY LOOKS at how the government holds corporate entities liable for criminal acts. The law recognizes the corporation as a person, but its actions are directed by people—the employees and directors who work for and on behalf of the business. The *Justice Manual,* a comprehensive policy guideline for United States Attorneys' Offices, notes that "prosecution of corporate crime is a high priority" and directs prosecutors to "focus on wrongdoing by individuals from the beginning of any investigation of corporate misconduct" (US DOJ, 2018, 9-28.010). The manual recognizes that "a corporation only acts through individuals" (US DOJ, 2018, 9-28.010). But in cases of white-collar crime, federal prosecutors can and do pursue criminal charges against corporate wrongdoing.

How does one punish a corporation? Mostly through monetary fines and increased oversight, often under terms negotiated between the government and the corporation. These settlements—either deferred prosecution agreements (DPAs) or nonprosecution agreements (NPAs)—are touted as efficient ways to resolve disputes, improve corporate compliance, increase the company's cooperation with the government's ongoing investigation, and control the collateral consequences that might affect innocent parties, such as the corporation's employees (Reilly, 2019). But critics argue that they can lead prosecutors to focus on institutional rather than individual misconduct, leave the impression that corporations can buy their way out of criminal charges, and shield important information about misconduct from the public, among other consequences (Reilly, 2019).

The criminal behavior in this case was General Motors' failure for about a decade to notify regulators of a product defect, namely, a faulty ignition switch that could cause a car to turn off while driving, which would incapacitate the

United States Department of Justice, *Justice Manual*

9-28.000. Principles of Federal Prosecution of Business Organizations

9-28.300. Factors to Be Considered

A. General Principle: Generally, prosecutors apply the same factors in determining whether to charge a corporation as they do with respect to individuals. . . . Thus, the prosecutor must weigh all of the factors normally considered in the sound exercise of prosecutorial judgment: the sufficiency of the evidence; the likelihood of success at trial; the probable deterrent, rehabilitative, and other consequences of conviction; and the adequacy of noncriminal approaches. However, due to the nature of the corporate "person," some additional factors are present. In conducting an investigation, determining whether to bring charges, and negotiating plea or other agreements, prosecutors should consider the following factors in reaching a decision as to the proper treatment of a corporate target:

1. the nature and seriousness of the offense, including the risk of harm to the public, and applicable policies and priorities, if any, governing the prosecution of corporations for particular categories of crime;

2. the pervasiveness of wrongdoing within the corporation, including the complicity in, or the condoning of, the wrongdoing by corporate management;

3. the corporation's history of similar misconduct, including prior criminal, civil, and regulatory enforcement actions against it;

4. the corporation's willingness to cooperate, including as to potential wrongdoing by its agents;

5. the adequacy and effectiveness of the corporation's compliance program at the time of the offense, as well as at the time of a charging decision;

6. the corporation's timely and voluntary disclosure of wrongdoing;

7. the corporation's remedial actions, including, but not limited to, any efforts to implement an adequate and effective corporate compliance program or to improve an existing one, to replace responsible management, to discipline or terminate wrongdoers, or to pay restitution;

8. collateral consequences, including whether there is disproportionate harm to shareholders, pension holders, employees, and
   others not proven personally culpable, as well as impact on the
   public arising from the prosecution;

9. the adequacy of remedies such as civil or regulatory enforcement actions, including remedies resulting from the corporation's cooperation with relevant government agencies; and

10. the adequacy of the prosecution of individuals responsible for
    the corporation's malfeasance.

B. Comment: The factors listed in this section are intended to be illus-
trative of those that should be evaluated and are not an exhaustive list
of potentially relevant considerations. Some of these factors may not
apply to specific cases, and in some cases one factor may override all
others. For example, the nature and seriousness of the offense may
be such as to warrant prosecution regardless of the other factors. In
most cases, however, no single factor will be dispositive. In addition,
national law enforcement policies in various enforcement areas may
require that more or less weight be given to certain of these factors
than to others. Of course, prosecutors must exercise their thoughtful
and pragmatic judgment in applying and balancing these factors, so
as to achieve a fair and just outcome and promote respect for the law.

airbags. The defect was linked to at least 124 deaths, plus numerous injuries
(Woodyard, 2015). Despite the wide range of harm and the extent of the cover-
up, no individuals were prosecuted for crimes relating to the faulty product.
While reading this case study on *United States v. General Motors, Inc.,* think
about whether this outcome is a deterrent to other corporations, corporate
employees, or company directors. Is there a better way to police corporate
misconduct? And how should the government treat the individuals involved
in corporate crimes?

THE SWITCH

In the early 2000s, General Motors released a series of vehicles marketed
toward first-time car buyers, including the Chevrolet Cobalt, the Pontiac G5
and Solstice, and the Saturn Ion, among other compact cars. They were

advertised as fuel-efficient, affordable, and safe (Deferred Prosecution Agreement, 2015, Exhibit C). But soon after the cars hit the road, GM began getting reports of a problem: drivers reported sudden stalls and engine shut-offs while driving. The problem appeared to stem from the ignition switch, which moved too easily out of the "run" position and into "accessory" or "off," cutting power to the steering and braking systems.

The ignition switch at issue was first developed in the late 1990s. Preproduction testing in 2001 and 2002 revealed that it wasn't meeting GM's own specifications for torque—the amount of pressure necessary to turn the key in the ignition. Despite internal reports that the switch turned off with only slight pressure to the key, the part was installed in the 2003 model year of the Saturn Ion and then in the Chevy Cobalt. When the cars were released, customers weren't the only ones noticing the problems. GM employees reported stalls while driving, with some blaming the too-easy rotation of the key in the ignition. Even reporters covering the Cobalt launch experienced the problem. The press reports prompted two GM safety executives to test-drive the car, and they too found that the car could be turned off if the driver's knee bumped the keys. In response, GM recommended that drivers remove "nonessential material from their key rings" (Deferred Prosecution Agreement, 2015, Exhibit C, p. 29).

General Motors, like other auto manufacturers, was required to disclose any defect relating to motor vehicle safety to the National Highway Traffic Safety Administration (NHTSA). Motor vehicle safety is defined as "performance of a motor vehicle ... in a way that protects the public against unreasonable risk of accidents ... and against unreasonable risk of death or injury in an accident" (49 USC §§ 30118(c)(1) and 30102(a)(8)). A safety disclosure must be submitted to NHTSA within five working days of the discovery of a safety-related defect.

In November 2004, GM considered a fix to the ignition switch, which had since been installed in the Pontiac Solstice. This was the first of six engineering inquiries over the following five years prompting the company to consider changes to new vehicles. This first attempt at a solution ended a few months later with no action, as did the subsequent inquiries. The GM engineers concluded in March 2005 that the switch did not pose a safety concern and that solutions to the issue would take too long to complete, would cost too much, and wouldn't completely solve the problem (Deferred Prosecution Agreement, 2015, Exhibit C, p. 30). At least one GM engineer disagreed, insisting the switch posed a safety concern because it could result in a sudden loss of power steering and brakes. But that view did not prevail. Just two months after the first inquiry closed, a GM brand quality manager opened a second inquiry into the issue to examine whether to address the problem for new cars. This inquiry was prompted by a customer complaint that the car's ignition would turn off while driving, and the manager noted that GM had to buy back Cobalts because of the ignition issue. Engineers proposed changing the design of the key head to address the problem, but the idea was rejected, and GM continued to install the ignition switch in new cars.

The company sent a service bulletin to dealers in 2005 notifying them that there could be a problem with the ignition inadvertently turning off, and instructed dealers to provide an insert for the key head to any customers who reported the problem. The insert would lessen the risk of inadvertent rotation of the ignition switch. The service bulletin purposely avoided use of the word *stall* to describe the problem, at the direction of a product investigations senior manager. While customers would naturally describe the problem as "stalling," that term might attract the attention of NHTSA, GM's regulator wrote (Deferred Prosecution Agreement, 2015, Exhibit C, pp. 31–32). But that meant a dealer's search for bulletins relating to stalls would come up empty. The service bulletin was later updated to cover 2007 model years of the Cobalt, Chevrolet HHR, Ion, and Solstice, as well as the Pursuit and Saturn Sky. In all, about 430 customers received the inserts for their keys between 2005 and 2014. In June 2005, GM acknowledged the ignition switch issue, but said that it did not believe that "inadvertent rotation of the ignition key was a safety issue" (Deferred Prosecution Agreement, 2015, Exhibit C, p. 26).

In April 2006, the GM design release engineer authorized a replacement of the defective ignition switch in new cars, changing to a switch that required significantly greater torque to turn the engine off. But the change was implemented without changing the part number, which went against GM's practices. Retaining the part number made it impossible to tell the difference between the defective switch and the new one without taking a switch apart to examine it.

While engineers focused on the problem of the ignition switch inadvertently cutting power to the steering and braking systems, few seemed to recognize that the loss of power to the electrical system could also affect the airbags (Deferred Prosecution Agreement, 2015, Exhibit C, p. 33). The loss of the electrical system would result in the "sensing diagnostic module" (SDM) being disabled. The SDM triggered the airbags to inflate in a collision. Without power to the SDM, the airbags would not deploy.

The deadly effect of the defective switch had been recorded as early as 2004, when a thirty-seven-year-old woman driving a Saturn Ion died when her airbags failed to deploy in a crash. Later the same year, Candice Anderson was driving her 2004 Saturn Ion when she inexplicably lost control and hit a tree (Ruiz, 2014). Her boyfriend, Gene Erickson, died at the scene. Anderson was charged with and pleaded guilty to negligent homicide, serving a five-year probation sentence. She also paid more than $10,000 in fines and restitution.

Other fatalities included the following:

In June 2005, a forty-year-old man suffered serious injuries after his 2005 Ion crashed and the airbags failed to deploy.

In July 2005, a sixteen-year-old driver died in Maryland when her 2005 Cobalt crashed and the airbags failed to deploy. Because the Cobalt's SDM recorded data about the crash, investigators confirmed that the ignition was in "accessory" mode.

In October 2006, two teenagers in Wisconsin died when their 2005 Cobalt crashed and the airbags failed to deploy. Police recorded that the ignition appeared to be in the "accessory" position.

NHTSA took note, asking GM about the high number of airbag nondeployments in Cobalts and Ions and specifically expressing concern over the July 2005 accident that killed the Maryland teenager. In response, GM assigned an employee to track reports of crashes in Cobalts where airbags failed to deploy, and in May 2007, the product investigations group placed the issue into the first stage of the recall process. But there was no follow-up and the issue did not move forward.

Meanwhile, there were more fatalities linked to the faulty ignition switch. Two people died in September 2008 when the airbags in their 2006 Cobalt failed to deploy in a crash. And in April 2009, a seventy-three-year-old woman and her thirteen-year-old granddaughter were killed when the ignition switch in her 2005 Cobalt slipped into the "accessory" position, disabling the airbags. The woman's great-grandson, the sole survivor of the crash, was paralyzed from the waist down. He was twelve months old.

In December 2009, there were two more crashes of Chevrolet Cobalts linked to the ignition switch issue. In Tennessee, a twenty-five-year-old nursing student died in a head-on collision in her 2006 Cobalt. The airbags did not deploy and the ignition was turned to the "off" position at the time of the crash. And a thirty-five-year-old woman in Virginia suffered a serious head injury and fractured ribs when the airbags in her 2005 Cobalt failed to inflate. Investigators found the ignition was in the "accessory" position. And in March 2010, a twenty-nine-year-old woman in Georgia died after her 2005 Cobalt lost power to the steering system.

These deaths and serious injuries were often followed by lawsuits against GM, civil suits brought by those harmed in accidents and the families of those killed. As early as 2011, some GM lawyers handling these claims saw a pattern in the nondeployment cases linked to an anomaly in the ignition switch. A GM engineer explained to the legal staff handling the 2009 Tennessee case, "When the ignition switch power mode status is in Off . . . the SDM 'powers down' and the airbags fail to deploy" (Deferred Prosecution Agreement, 2015, Exhibit C, p. 35). This link between the ignition switch and airbag failure raised a risk of punitive damages, and GM settled the Tennessee case three months later.

The attorney in charge of handling the airbag claims believed the problem wasn't getting sufficient attention from the product investigations group, which was supposed to find solutions to problems that cars had on the road. In July 2011, the legal department took the unusual step of meeting with the product investigations group to share the pattern of airbags failing in accidents where the ignition was turned to "accessory" or "off." As of that time, the GM working groups hadn't yet linked the power failure to the defective ignition switch torque. GM engineers undertook a more concerted investigation of the airbag nondeployment problem in mid-March 2012.

Within two weeks, members of the GM electrical engineering group traveled to a salvage yard to study electrical problems associated with the ignition switch, following up on the legal team's concerns. One of the engineers noticed the low torque in a 2006 Cobalt's ignition and confirmed that suspicion by using a fish scale from a local bait-and-tackle shop. A month later, a second trip to a salvage yard with more sophisticated equipment validated the finding that the majority of cars from model years 2003 to 2007 had ignition switches with torque that measured below GM's specifications. This discovery led the group to research customer complaints and the 2005 service bulletin addressing the low resistance in the ignition switch. A GM electrical engineer reported to his boss that the defective switch was the likely cause of airbag nondeployment. That report made its way through several layers of supervisors, but not into the formal recall process. Various safety personnel, legal representatives, and other managers met throughout 2012 and 2013 to discuss possible solutions to the defective switch.

But at the same time the investigation was bouncing between work groups and stalling in the process, GM employees met with NHTSA officials to assure regulators that its product recall system was efficient, describing a streamlined procedure that allowed the company to respond quickly to potential safety issues. At the time of the NHTSA meeting, it had been five months since GM personnel had identified a dangerous safety defect, and the problem had not yet hit the first stage of the recall process.

Accident victims continued to file lawsuits against GM, and in April 2013, a plaintiff's attorney took the deposition of a GM design release engineer about the ignition switch, showing the engineer X-rays of the vehicle in the Georgia crash and comparing that to a later-model Cobalt. When confronted with the physical differences in the ignition switches, the engineer denied any knowledge of a change to the mechanism. But soon after his deposition, the engineer realized that there had indeed been a design change after model year 2005, which he confirmed by taking apart ignition switches from 2005 and a later model. He told two supervisors about his findings, but was told to let the attorneys handle the matter.

Still, GM did not move toward a recall. In June 2013, a twenty-three-year-old man died in Quebec after his 2007 Cobalt ran off the road and into some trees. The airbag failed to deploy and the ignition was turned to "accessory."

The ignition switch issue finally entered GM's internal recall process in November 2013, after 804 days of formal investigation. During this same period, GM was meeting with NHTSA to assure the regulator that the company was addressing safety defects swiftly. The regulator did not know of the ignition switch issue, though it had raised concerns about the airbag failures.

On January 31, 2014, GM decided to conduct a recall for the defective ignition switch, and informed NHTSA on February 7. The vehicles subject to the recall were older and many were no longer in production. Approximately eight hundred consumers had purchased certified preowned vehicles with the faulty ignition switch, and GM had given those vehicles a safety certification—even after the company became aware of the defective part.

The government estimated that GM missed the five-day regulatory reporting requirement by twenty months and noted that the knowledge of the defective parts went far higher in the organization than the investigating engineers—extending up to GM's safety director and the GM safety attorney. The recall covered some 2 million vehicles.

THE RESOLUTION

The NHTSA's internal investigation was over, but the government's investigation was just getting started. Multiple federal agencies, including transportation agencies and the FBI, worked on the investigation into whether GM's making false statements to regulators and withholding safety concerns in violation of NHTSA regulations amounted to criminal conduct. In September 2015, the US Attorney's Office in the Southern District of New York announced that GM had entered into a deferred prosecution agreement (DPA) with the government. GM admitted that it failed to disclose safety defects to consumers and regulators. The company agreed to forfeit $900 million to the government as a penalty.

A DPA is a contract between the US Attorney's Office and the defendant in which the defendant corporation admits wrongdoing and agrees to pay a fine and improve its internal compliance standards and procedures. In return, the prosecutor files an information charging the defendant with criminal violations but holds the criminal case in abeyance for a specified time to permit the defendant to meet the terms of the DPA. Once the terms are met, the government agrees to dismiss the charges.

In GM's case, the government filed a two-count information, charging the company with making false statements to regulators, a violation of 18 U.S.C. § 1001, and wire fraud, in violation of 18 U.S.C. § 1343. Count 1 alleged that GM engaged in a scheme to conceal potentially deadly safety defects from NHTSA, which it was required to disclose within five business days. Count 2 alleged that GM engaged in a scheme to defraud in 2012 and 2013 by continuing to sell GM-certified preowned vehicles that were equipped with a defective ignition switch. The government alleged that the company made representations about the safety of those cars over the internet, certifying that the cars had been checked for safety, including the ignition system, and that the company withheld material information that it had a duty to disclose—namely, that the cars had a defective ignition switch.

In a twenty-page statement, GM accepted responsibility and detailed in a timeline how engineers and executives became aware of the defect and failed

18 U.S.C. § 1001. Statement or Entries Generally

(a) Except as otherwise provided in this section, whoever, in any matter within the jurisdiction of the executive, legislative, or judicial branch of the Government of the United States, knowingly and willfully—

(1) falsifies, conceals, or covers up by any trick, scheme, or device a material fact;

(2) makes any materially false, fictitious, or fraudulent statement or representation; or

(3) makes or uses any false writing or document knowing the same to contain any materially false, fictitious, or fraudulent statement or entry;
   shall be fined under this title, imprisoned not more than 5 years or, if the offense involves international or domestic terrorism (as defined in section 2331), imprisoned not more than 8 years, or both. . . .

Federal Rules of Criminal Procedure, Rule 48. Dismissal (*nolle prosequi*)

(a) By the Government. The government may, with leave of court, dismiss an indictment, information, or complaint. The government may not dismiss the prosecution during trial without the defendant's consent.

(b) By the Court. The court may dismiss an indictment, information, or complaint if unnecessary delay occurs in:
   (1) presenting a charge to a grand jury;
   (2) filing an information against a defendant; or
   (3) bringing a defendant to trial.

to inform regulators and consumers. GM agreed to continue to cooperate with the federal investigation as requested.

The government agreed to defer prosecution for three years, during which time an independent monitor would review and assess the adequacy and effectiveness of GM's policies, practices, and procedures for addressing safety issues and recalls, sharing information among all work groups, and addressing defects in certified preowned vehicles.

On the same day that the DPA was announced, GM said that it was setting aside $575 million to settle more than thirteen hundred civil lawsuits relating to deaths and injuries linked to the defective part. A law firm hired by GM to assess claims and compensate victims estimated that 124 deaths were related to the ignition switch problem.

Beyond the injuries and deaths, several drivers suffered criminal convictions relating to the accidents. Ten years after Candice Anderson lost her boyfriend when her Saturn Ion hit a tree, a judge cleared her record, erasing the conviction for criminally negligent homicide (Ruiz, 2014). Five months prior to Candace's 2007 guilty plea, GM had reviewed the crash and determined that the car was to blame, a fact not revealed until the recall was announced in 2014.

Other drivers also were charged criminally for accidents later linked to the defective ignition switch (Green and Cronin Fisk, 2015). An eighteen-year-old man lost control of his car and went off the road in Camillus, New York, in May 2006, killing his passenger. The airbags didn't inflate. The driver was convicted of negligent homicide and spent six months in jail. In 2011, a nineteen-year-old man lost control of his mother's 2007 Saturn as he drove to Bible study outside Houston, Texas, crossed into oncoming traffic, and hit a pickup head-on, killing the driver. The Saturn driver suffered a brain injury that left him without a memory of the accident. He was arrested and charged with manslaughter in 2014. His investigator linked the accident to GM's recall defect and the charges were dropped after eight months. In most of the cases where drivers were criminally charged, GM has privately settled civil lawsuits with the drivers and the families of those killed in the accidents.

THE CRITICS

The negotiated settlement drew many critics, including US senators Richard Blumenthal (D-Conn.) and Edward J. Markey (D-Mass.), who called it "extremely disappointing" that the company would not be "held fully accountable for their wrongdoings" (Harwell, 2015). The DPA was criticized for being disproportionate to a prior government settlement with Toyota, which paid $1.2 billion for failing to disclose defects that caused unintended acceleration in its cars and was linked to five deaths (Harwell, 2015). And the fine itself, $900 million, was a fraction of GM's $156 billion in revenue in 2014.

Further, critics noted that the DPA conflicted with the US Department of Justice policy that urged prosecutors to focus on investigating and punishing employees, not just companies, in white-collar cases (Yates, 2015). That policy was announced by then deputy attorney general Sally Yates in a speech in which she said, "Crime is crime. And it is our obligation at the Justice Department to ensure that we are holding lawbreakers accountable regardless of whether they commit their crimes on the street corner or in the boardroom" (Yates, 2015). The revised policy for investigating corporate wrongdoing required companies to disclose the responsible employees in order to receive credit for cooperation in a federal criminal prosecution. Yates insisted that "we're not going to let corporations plead ignorance. If they don't know who is responsible, they will need to find out" (Yates, 2015).

In announcing the GM deal, Preet Bharara, the US attorney for the Southern District of New York, credited the company with "fairly extraordinary" cooperation in the investigation once the defect was revealed (Henning, 2015). GM fired fifteen people, including eight executives, over the ignition switch issue (Shepardson, 2018). Yet no GM employees were charged with wrongdoing.

The criminal charges were dismissed in September 2018 after GM completed the three-year monitoring period. The company said that it had made substantial safety improvements and added a new product safety structure (Shepardson, 2018).

The US Department of Justice has since revised its white-collar criminal enforcement policies under a new administration (Rosenstein, 2017). Deputy Attorney General Rod Rosenstein said in 2017 that the "notion that companies should be required to locate and report to the government every person involved in alleged misconduct in any way regardless of their role, may sound reasonable. . . . But consider cases in which the government alleges that routine activities of many employees of a large corporation were part of an illegal scheme" (Rosenstein, 2017). It's not practical to require the company to locate and report every employee, he said, when the allegations involve "activities throughout the company over a long period of time."

Deferred prosecution agreements reflect the reality that corporate defendants have leverage to negotiate a resolution of a criminal case in ways that an individual does not (Reilly, 2019). If punished too severely, a corporate entity can file for bankruptcy protection, which can harm employees and shareholders. A corporation can relocate to a more business-friendly jurisdiction. It can also do as GM did here and offer to create special restitution funds to compensate victims as part of the plea-bargaining process. And in most cases where a corporate defendant's case is resolved with a deferred prosecution or nonprosecution agreement, no employees are prosecuted (Garrett, 2015).

REFERENCES

Deferred Prosecution Agreement. (2015). United States v. General Motors, Inc. 15-cr-00747. S. Dist. New York. November 17.

Department of Justice. (2015). Manhattan U.S. Attorney Announces Criminal Charges Against General Motors and Deferred Prosecution Agreement with $900 Million Forfeiture. September 17. https://www.justice.gov/usao-sdny/pr/manhattan-us-attorney-announces-criminal-charges-against-general-motors-and-deferred.

Garrett, B. (2015). "The Corporate Criminal as Scapegoat." *Virginia Law Review* 101, no. 7 (November).

Gibson Dunn. (2019). "2018 Year-End Update on Corporate Non-prosecution and Deferred Prosecution Agreements." January 10. https://www.gibsondunn.com/2018-year-end-npa-dpa-update/.

Green, J., and M. Cronin Fisk. (2015). "Drivers Convicted, Jailed for Crashes Now Blamed on Car Defects." *Insurance Journal,* September 2. https://www.insurancejournal.com/news/national/2015/09/02/380369.htm.

Harwell, D. (2015). "Why General Motors' $900 Million Fine for a Deadly Defect Is Just a Slap on the Wrist." *Washington Post,* September 17. https://www.washingtonpost.com/news/business/wp/2015/09/17/why-general-motors-900-million-fine-for-a-deadly-defect-is-just-a-slap-on-the-wrist/.

Henning, P. (2015). "Many Messages in the G.M. Settlement." *New York Times,* September 21. https://www.nytimes.com/2015/09/22/business/dealbook/many-messages-in-the-gm-settlement.html.

Reilly, P. (2019). "Sweetheart Deals, Deferred Prosecution, and Making a Mockery of the Criminal Justice System: U.S. Corporate DPAs Rejected on Many Fronts." *Arizona State Law Journal* 50, no. 4 (winter): 1113.

Rosenstein, R. (2017). "Excerpt of Remarks by Deputy Attorney General Rod Rosenstein at 34th International Conference on the Foreign Corrupt Practices Act." United States Department of Justice. November 29. https://www.justice.gov/opa/speech/deputy-attorney-general-rosenstein-delivers-remarks-34th-international-conference-foreign.

Ruiz, R. (2014). "Woman Cleared in a Death Tied to GM's Faulty Ignition Switch." *New York Times*, November 24.

Shepardson, D. (2018). "U.S. Judge Dismisses GM Ignition Switch Criminal Case." Reuters, September 19. https://www.reuters.com/article/us-gm-ignition/u-s-judge-dismisses-gm-ignition-switch-criminal-case-idUSKCN1LZ2U0#.

US DOJ (United States Justice Department). (2018). *Justice Manual.* 9-28.010. Foundational Principles of Corporate Prosecution. Updated 2018. (Formerly known as *United States Attorneys Manual*). https://www.justice.gov/jm/justice-manual.

Woodyard, C. (2015). "GM Ignition Switch Deaths Hit 124." *USA Today*, July 13. https://www.usatoday.com/story/money/cars/2015/07/13/gm-ignition-switch-death-toll/30092693/.

Yates, S. (2015). "Deputy Attorney General Sally Quillian Yates Delivers Remarks at New York University School of Law Announcing New Policy on Individual Liability in Matters of Corporate Wrongdoing." United States Department of Justice. September 10. https://www.justice.gov/opa/speech/deputy-attorney-general-sally-quillian-yates-delivers-remarks-new-york-university-school.

SEVEN

Money Laundering

*UNITED STATES V. LIBERTY RESERVE, S.A.,
ARTHUR BUDOVSKY, ET AL.*

THE OBJECT OF MOST FINANCIAL crimes is to make a profit, but that profit can create another problem: how to get illicit proceeds of criminal activity into the legitimate economic system so the money can easily be spent. The term for converting the proceeds of crime into funds that are "clean" is called money laundering. The process of laundering funds involves three steps (1) *placement* of the dirty money into the legitimate financial system; (2) concealing the source of the funds by *layering* transactions, thus moving the money in order to distance it from its illegal source; and then *integrating* the proceeds into the lawful monetary system by using them to buy legitimate assets.

A narcotics trafficker cannot just walk into a bank to deposit hundreds of thousands of dollars in cash without raising a few eyebrows—and generating a currency transaction report, which is mandated under the Bank Secrecy Act of 1970. Under that law, banks are required to report any cash transaction over $10,000, properly identify the person conducting the transaction, and maintain a record of it (31 U.S.C. § 5313). But breaking that large bag of cash into smaller deposits to avoid the reporting limit is called structuring, and that is a federal crime (31 U.S.C. § 5324). The bank is also required to identify transactions that appear suspicious, such as sequential deposits that are just below the reporting limit (31. C.F.R. [Code of Federal Regulations] § 103.18). Banks, and other financial institutions to which these laws apply, are required to have anti–money laundering systems in place, such as "know your customer" (KYC) procedures that ensure the bank has identified the individual who is conducting the transaction.

Congress passed the Money Laundering Control Act in 1986, making it a crime to conduct a monetary transaction knowing that the funds were the proceeds of a crime. The element of "knowing" is met when a defendant is "willfully blind" to the source of the money or does not exercise reasonable care expected in a financial transaction (Albanese, 2011, p. 110). Anti–money laundering laws have evolved to include more than just banks, covering check-cashing companies, money transmitters, pawnbrokers, casinos, credit card companies, jewelers, and others.

Traditionally, money laundering might include smuggling bulk cash or converting cash into other forms, such as money orders, casino chips, art, or jewelry. But increasingly, money laundering is going online where digital currency can provide anonymity and easy movement of illegal funds. Virtual currency or cryptocurrency, such as Bitcoin and Litecoin, is digital money that takes the form of tokens (FinCEN, 2013). The US Department of the Treasury's Financial Crimes Enforcement Network (FinCEN) enforces anti–money laundering regulations on virtual currencies, but its reach can be frustrated by the anonymity of the internet.

This case study examines the case of Liberty Reserve, a digital currency exchange that promised its users anonymity and marketed itself to a criminal clientele that laundered $6 billion in illicit proceeds. As you read this chapter, think about the challenges that financial regulators and law enforcement faced in this case and how what they learned can aid future investigations.

THE CRIME

Law enforcement began watching online money transmitting services in 2003 while conducting an undercover operation that targeted a website called Shadowcrew (Zetter, 2013). That site was a forum for "carders," hackers who steal, buy, and sell stolen credit card data (see chapter 5, "Cybercrime"). In one cyberheist, stolen credit card and debit card numbers were encoded on blank cards, which were then used to siphon money from ATMs. The proceeds were channeled back to former Soviet bloc countries using a service called E-Gold. It was the hackers' preferred method of transferring money because they could do so anonymously.

Money transmitters like Western Union that offer services within the United States are required to comply with regulations, including a requirement to authenticate the identity of customers and to file "suspicious activity reports" on transactions that appear to have violated the law. E-Gold tried to skirt that law by calling itself a payment system, not a money transmitter. But this characterization did not deter federal law enforcement. E-Gold's founder, Douglas Jackson, pleaded guilty in 2008 to money-laundering charges and to operating an unlicensed money-transmitting service. Then the federal government mined E-Gold's servers and files to build cases against some of the most wanted carders and hackers.

Around the same time that E-Gold was operating, Arthur Budovsky, a Costa Rican citizen of Ukrainian origin, started up a similar operation, GoldAge, with his partner Vladimir Kats (Government's Sentencing Submission, 2016). GoldAge was a digital currency exchange operating out of Brooklyn, New York. In 2006, Budovsky and Kats were indicted for operating an illegal money-transmitting business operation. They both pleaded guilty and were sentenced to 5 years' probation. By the time they were sentenced on that conviction, they had already launched their next digital currency exchange—Liberty Reserve. This time, they went offshore, incorporating and opening bank accounts in Costa Rica, though they operated the business from their homes in Brooklyn.

Budovsky knew that digital currency exchanges were popular with internet investment schemes known as high-yield investment programs (HYIPs), which, as he understood, were nothing but Ponzi schemes. He and Kats designed Liberty Reserve to attract HYIPs and other online criminals, such as carders and identity thieves. Liberty Reserve had weak anti–money laundering controls and quickly became known as an easy way to anonymously transfer money. To open an account, customers needed only a valid email address. Name, address, and date of birth were required, but these weren't validated, so users could open accounts under fake names or stolen identities (Government's Sentencing Submission, 2016). Liberty Reserve charged a 1 percent fee on each transaction. For 75 cents, a user could hide his or her account number in the transaction (Indictment, 2013). That anonymity spurred Liberty Reserve's growth to more than 1 million users worldwide, with the enterprise processing 12 million transactions a year and becoming a favored money-laundering service in the criminal underworld.

In a study of online money-laundering techniques for the United Nations Office on Drugs and Crime (UNODC), Jean-Loup Richet (2013) found that Liberty Reserve developed a reputation among hackers and carders reliably keeping transactions anonymous, but that it also attracted some "dodgy" characters (p. 3). In an online forum, one participant characterized Liberty Reserve as "for scammers and scammed people" (p. 3). But it was touted as the place to go for laundering money. A forum member assured another that "the reason Liberty Reserve is used, is cause [*sic*] no information is needed to be entered thus making it 100% anonymous" (Richet, 2013, p. 3). Another said that "no one can send money directly to/from them. I guess that's the beauty of what makes it 100% anonymous. They don't have any of your info. Only the exchangers you use" (Richet, 2013, p. 4).

Liberty Reserve users could not deposit or withdraw funds directly. Rather, they were required to purchase and redeem LR, Liberty Reserve's digital currency, using third-party exchangers (Government's Sentencing Submission, 2016). An exchanger could buy and sell LR in bulk from Liberty Reserve, and it could then buy and sell that e-currency in smaller transactions in exchange for traditional currency. Upon receiving payment, the exchanger credited the user's Liberty Reserve account with the corresponding amount, transferring LR from the exchanger's Liberty Reserve account to the user's account. When the user wanted to withdraw funds, they were required to transfer LR from their Liberty Reserve account to the exchanger's account, and the exchanger would make arrangements to transfer mainstream currency to the user. Exchangers took a 5 percent fee for each transaction, far more than a regulated bank would charge. The exchangers typically operated in areas with little regulation or oversight, such as Malaysia, Russia, Nigeria, and Vietnam (Indictment, 2013).

Liberty Reserve also offered a "shopping cart interface" that merchant websites could install to accept LR as payment for their products. But participating merchants were "overwhelmingly criminal in nature" (Indictment, 2013, p. 9). Those using the shopping cart interface included credit card data traffickers, online Ponzi schemes, hackers for hire, gambling enterprises, and underground drug-dealing websites. Budovsky, Kats, and their partners understood that Liberty Reserve was breaking the law. In online chat records, Kats noted that it was well known that "LR is [a] money-laundering operation that hackers use" (Indictment, 2013, p. 10).

In 2007, Budovsky traveled to Costa Rica to set up Liberty Reserve's office. He decided to move there permanently in 2008 and obtain citizenship. He also began to push Kats out of the business, using as leverage his control over Liberty Reserve's domain name and infrastructure. He eventually agreed to buy Kats's share of Liberty Reserve for $200,000, though they would remain partners in several other businesses.

Budovsky applied to register with Costa Rica's regulatory authority, the Superintendencia General de Entidades Financieras (SUGEF), but without revealing his role in the company or the identity of the company's clients. On the application, Ahmed Yassine was listed as the owner, with power of attorney,

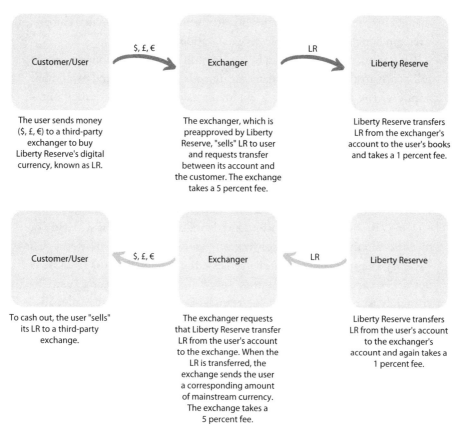

FIGURE 7.1. Liberty Reserve users did not buy or sell LR, the digital currency, directly with the company, but were required to go through third-party exchangers. Users often used blatantly fictional identifications to set up Liberty Reserve accounts, such as "Joe Bogus," the name used by an undercover agent during the investigation (Government's Sentencing Submission, 2016, p. 5). Liberty Reserve customers buying and selling goods using LR thus gained an additional layer of anonymity, as the their real names were known only to the third-party exchangers.

and the sole legal representative. Budovsky thus concealed his criminal convictions for having run an unlicensed money-transmitting business.

SUGEF requested information about Liberty Reserve's anti–money laundering controls, such as its "know your customer" procedures, but Budovsky claimed that its only customers were the third-party exchangers. The exchangers, Budovsky said, were responsible for verifying its customers—the end users. SUGEF insisted on more robust controls and that Liberty Reserve implement changes that would permit its detection of money-laundering activities by the exchangers. Budovsky had no intention to adopt changes that put his clientele at risk, but he did hire a general manager, Marco Cubero, a veteran banker with an impeccable reputation.

Cubero and Budovsky began to clash within a short time. Cubero wanted full access to the company's data and records so he could understand the nature of the transactions. But Budovsky said no. Cubero drafted anti–money laundering controls and programs, but Budovsky delayed their implementation. Cubero sought to implement a suspicious activity alert system, but that, too, was denied. To throw off Cubero and the Costa Rican authorities, Budovsky created a portal that allowed the general manager and regulators to monitor transactions, but the portal he set up for them was fed fake transactions. By mid-2011, SUGEF advised Liberty Reserve that because of ongoing problems with the anti–money laundering controls, it still had not met the requirements for registration. Around the same time, the US Treasury Department's Financial Crimes Enforcement Network (FinCEN) notified financial institutions that Liberty Reserve was being "used by criminals to conduct anonymous transactions to move money globally" (Indictment, 2013). Two weeks after Budovsky learned of the notice, he told the Costa Rican authorities that the business had been sold to a foreign company and would no longer be operating out of Costa Rica.

Budovsky crafted a plan to sell Liberty Reserve to a company in Cyprus—a company that he controlled. Using this shell company, he "purchased" Liberty Reserve. He then transferred Liberty Reserve's money out of Costa Rica through shell companies in Hong Kong, Russia, and Cyprus. However, the company continued to operate out of its offices in Costa Rica.

THE PROSECUTION

Liberty Reserve continued to thrive until May 2013, when federal agents arrested Budovsky and six others in what the United States law enforcement agents called a $6 billion money-laundering scheme. Budovsky was arrested in Spain, while others were arrested in New York and Costa Rica. Police in Costa Rica raided three homes and five businesses associated with Liberty Reserve. The site went off-line, its home page replaced by a notice that the domain had been seized by the United States Global Illicit Financial Team, which led the investigation. The Global Illicit Financial Team consists of Homeland Security Investigations (HSI), part of US Immigration and Customs Enforcement (ICE); the US Secret Service; and the IRS.

Along with Budovsky, other defendants in the case included Vladimir Kats, his former business partner and cofounder of Liberty Reserve; Azzeddine El Amine, a manager; and Mark Marmilev and Maxim Chukharev, who helped design and maintain Liberty Reserve's technological infrastructure (Indictment, 2013). The company itself was also named as a defendant.

Liberty Reserve had become a "financial hub of the cyber-crime world, facilitating a broad range of online criminal activity, including credit card fraud, identity theft, investment fraud, computer hacking, child pornography, and narcotics trafficking" (Indictment, 2013, p. 4). From 2006 to May 2013, Liberty Reserve had processed 55 million financial transactions, with an estimated $6 billion in criminal proceeds flowing through its system.

The indictment charged the defendants with money laundering (18 U.S.C. § 1956(a)(2)(B)(i)), conspiracy to operate unlicensed money-transmitting business (18 U.S.C. § 371), and operation of an unlicensed money-transmitting business (18 U.S.C. § 1960) and sought the forfeiture of $6 billion, including the funds held in specified bank accounts. The indictment also sought the forfeiture of the domain names that had been used in the operation.

More than a year after the indictment was unsealed and Budovsky was arrested, he was extradited from Spain to New York City. He had gone to great lengths to avoid US authorities, said Assistant Attorney General Leslie R. Caldwell. "He even renounced his US citizenship to try to escape facing justice in an American court room," Caldwell said in a press release (DOJ OPA, 2014). Four of Budovsky's codefendants had already pleaded guilty and were awaiting sentencing. Budovsky was arraigned on October 14, 2014, and pleaded not guilty. Budovsky was appointed counsel under the Criminal Justice Act. Federal prosecutors advised the court that there was an extraordinary amount of discovery in the case, that is, the evidence that the government may use at trial. To provide it to the defendant would require twenty-six two-terabyte hard drives, and downloading all the material onto the drives would take about two weeks to (Transcript, Arraignment, 2014, p. 6).

In November 2014, the court appointed new counsel to represent Budovsky—a team of six lawyers, four of whom had specialized experience in technology or with cases that had complex electronic discovery materials. A paralegal and an investigator assisted legal counsel as the team prepared for a February 2016 jury trial (Opinion and Order, 2019).

Three days before trial was set to start, Budovsky changed his plea. Pursuant to a plea agreement with the government, he pleaded guilty to one count—conspiracy to commit money laundering (Government's Sentencing Submission, 2016). Both sides agreed that the United States Sentencing Guidelines calculated Budovsky's sentence at 20 years' imprisonment, the statutory maximum sentence. Without the statutory cap, his potential sentence would be 30 years to life in prison, largely due to the hundreds of millions of dollars in criminal proceeds that Liberty Reserve laundered for US-based criminal enterprises.

The prosecutors argued that the 20-year sentence was warranted because Budovsky was the founder and leader of Liberty Reserve and was responsible for running a money-laundering operation "of unprecedented size and scope, which became the financial hub for cyber criminals around the world who used it to launder billions of dollars of criminal proceeds" (Government's Sentencing Submission, 2016, p. 2). Budovsky's personal earnings were difficult to estimate. He moved more than $25 million out of the Liberty Reserve system into accounts that he controlled, but did so using a complex network of third-party accounts. The government estimated that he moved $20 million to Hong Kong and China, and from there a portion of the money was layered through two accounts in Cyprus and from there to four other Cyprus accounts.

In addition, Budovsky had previously been convicted of running a similar operation, and had made his living through such illegal enterprises for most of his life. Also, the government stressed, Budovsky had minimized his own conduct and had shown no remorse for his actions.

The government pointed to Budovsky and Kats's history of fraud and money-laundering schemes going back to 1999. The two men registered a 501(c)(3) organization in 2000 called United Support for Humanity, a charitable organization that aimed to improve the lives of children with birth defects, disease, blindness, and poverty (Government's Sentencing Submission, 2016, pp. 7–8). Prosecutors said that the charity accepted checks from "donors" and deposited them into its bank account, and then Budovsky and Kats would simply return the donations as cash, minus a commission. The donors used the fraudulent tax write-off to conceal money from the IRS.

The government also alleged that for several years in the early 2000s, Budovsky and Kats laundered money for crooked medical clinics in Brooklyn and Queens in a scheme involving no-fault auto insurance fraud (Government's Sentencing Submission, 2016, p. 8). Prosecutors asserted that these two schemes, his prior conviction for running E-Gold, and his lack of remorse for his current crime demonstrated that Budovsky was a high risk for reoffending, which justified the longest possible sentence. Budovsky denied that the charitable organization was a sham, and denied involvement with fraudulent medical services or insurance fraud (Transcript, Sentencing Hearing, 2016, pp. 26–27).

Budovsky's lawyers argued that his sentence should be no more than 15 years, as that would be sufficient punishment for this "complex individual" (Defendant's Sentencing Submission, 2016, p. 2). "If we simply reduce Arthur Budovsky to the single story of his offense, we take away all of his humanity. That is not the aim of sentencing. Indeed, the aim of sentencing is to view the entire person. The goal of sentencing is to find the right balance among what at times may be conflicting narratives" (Defendant's Sentencing Submission, 2016, p. 2). Budovsky had many good qualities and was described by friends and family as caring, kind, generous, and charitable. In Costa Rica, he was known for his generosity to poor, homeless, and orphaned children. Complicating his circumstances was the fact that when his sentence ends, "he will be removed from the United States, possibly to Costa Rica, where he is a citizen but has no family," and he will be a man without a country. Considering that Budovsky had been in custody since 2013, he was essentially asking for a 10-year sentence.

The judge agreed with the government that Budovsky was a risk for recidivism. "I don't find any genuine remorse expressed to me. I don't find any heartfelt acknowledgment of the depth of criminality, the widespread impact or the enormity of what he did. I find submissions that attempt to shift blame: shift blame to Mr. Kats, shift blame to the victims of the various frauds, ultimately whose money was laundered by the people who stole from them or defrauded them through the Liberty Reserve system. In the face of overwhelming evidence of criminal intent and a massive complex criminal scheme, he's chosen to quibble around the edges" (Transcript, Sentencing Hearing, 2016, pp. 52–53).

The ultimate victim in money-laundering cases is society at large, but victims of some of the HYIP or online Ponzi schemes submitted letters to the court to describe how Liberty Reserve's crimes had affected them. A janitor who invested and lost $6,000 in such a scheme wrote, "I thought I was investing safely with professionals, not knowing I was in a lion's den. Until now my wife has not forgiven me. Part of the investment was her money. This crime has broken me down financially." (Government's Sentencing Submission, 2016, p. 45). Another victim said, "I'm embarrassed I believed that the opportunity to gain this much of a return on my money could ever happen. Due to a number of health issues creating a need for such a windfall on investment seemed like at the time a possible solution for my needs faced with my economic dilemma. I should have known it was too good to be true" (Government's Sentencing Submission, 2016, p. 45).

When the government seized Liberty Reserve, its users lost the LR in their accounts, and many took to online criminal forums to complain of losses of tens of thousands of dollars or more. But of the 5 million registered accounts on Liberty Reserve, only fifty people contacted the US Attorney's Office for the Southern District of New York, and those all appeared to be victims of online schemes that Liberty Reserve enabled and supported (Government's Sentencing Submission, 2016). One exchanger contacted prosecutors, but did not pursue a claim.

The many layers of deception Budovsky undertook while operating Liberty Reserve served as another indication to the court that he was likely to reoffend without a lengthy sentence. The court said, "I think there is enormous importance to deterring him from returning to this kind of fraudulent activity" (Transcript, Sentencing Hearing, 2016, p. 53). It was also important, the court believed, to consider general deterrence in this case: "The challenges are enormous in this digital age of having effective law enforcement in this kind of e-currency market and money-laundering scheme" (p. 54).

The judge imposed the sentence of 20 years imprisonment, a fine of $500,000, and a money judgment of $122 million. Budovsky will be deported upon his release from federal custody in 2030.

MONEY LAUNDERING AND DIGITAL CURRENCIES

Digital currencies, such as Bitcoin and others, and offshore payment processors continue to flourish as conduits for illicit proceeds of crime. The United Nation's Office on Drugs and Crime estimates that the amount of money laundered each year is between 2 and 5 percent of global GDP—or between $800 billion and $2 trillion (UNODC, 2019). Where once criminals invested in precious metals, channeled money through casinos, smuggled bulk cash, or created fraudulent invoices, they now have a whole new option—one that is easier to use and harder to detect (*Economist,* 2018). Experts believe that the use of digital currency to launder money represents a fraction of that amount, perhaps 3 to 4 percent, but an amount that is growing (*Economist,* 2018).

18 U.S.C. § 1956. Laundering of Monetary Instruments

(a)

(1) Whoever, knowing that the property involved in a financial transaction represents the proceeds of some form of unlawful activity, conducts or attempts to conduct such a financial transaction which in fact involves the proceeds of specified unlawful activity—
(A)

> (i) with the intent to promote the carrying on of specified unlawful activity; or

> (ii) with intent to engage in conduct constituting a violation of section 7201 or 7206 of the Internal Revenue Code of 1986; or

(B) knowing that the transaction is designed in whole or in part—

> (i) to conceal or disguise the nature, the location, the source, the ownership, or the control of the proceeds of specified unlawful activity; or

> (ii) to avoid a transaction reporting requirement under State or Federal law, shall be sentenced to a fine of not more than $500,000 or twice the value of the property involved in the transaction, whichever is greater, or imprisonment for not more than twenty years, or both. For purposes of this paragraph, a financial transaction shall be considered to be one involving the proceeds of specified unlawful activity if it is part of a set of parallel or dependent transactions, any one of which involves the proceeds of specified unlawful activity, and all of which are part of a single plan or arrangement.

(2) Whoever transports, transmits, or transfers, or attempts to transport, transmit, or transfer a monetary instrument or funds from a place in the United States to or through a place outside the United States or to a place in the United States from or through a place outside the United States—

(A) with the intent to promote the carrying on of specified unlawful activity; or

(B) knowing that the monetary instrument or funds involved in the transportation, transmission, or transfer represent the proceeds of some form of unlawful activity and knowing that such transportation, transmission, or transfer is designed in whole or in part—

   (i) to conceal or disguise the nature, the location, the source, the ownership, or the control of the proceeds of specified unlawful activity; or

  (ii) to avoid a transaction reporting requirement under State or Federal law,

    shall be sentenced to a fine of not more than $500,000 or twice the value of the monetary instrument or funds involved in the transportation, transmission, or transfer, whichever is greater, or imprisonment for not more than twenty years, or both. . . .

(3) Whoever, with the intent—

(A) to promote the carrying on of specified unlawful activity;

(B) to conceal or disguise the nature, location, source, ownership, or control of property believed to be the proceeds of specified unlawful activity; or

(C) to avoid a transaction reporting requirement under State or Federal law,

    conducts or attempts to conduct a financial transaction involving property represented to be the proceeds of specified unlawful activity, or property used to conduct or facilitate specified unlawful activity, shall be fined under this title or imprisoned for not more than 20 years, or both. For purposes of this paragraph and paragraph (2), the term "represented" means any representation made by a law enforcement officer or by another person at the direction of, or with the approval of, a Federal official authorized to investigate or prosecute violations of this section.

(b) Penalties.—

(1) In general.—Whoever conducts or attempts to conduct a transaction described in subsection (a)(1) or (a)(3), or section 1957, or a transportation, transmission, or transfer described in subsection (a)(2), is liable to the United States for a civil penalty of not more than the greater of—

(A) the value of the property, funds, or monetary instruments involved in the transaction; or

(B) $10,000.

(2) Jurisdiction over foreign persons.—For purposes of adjudicating an action filed or enforcing a penalty ordered under this section, the district courts shall have jurisdiction over any foreign person, including any financial institution authorized under the laws of a foreign country, against whom the action is brought, if service of process upon the foreign person is made under the Federal Rules of Civil Procedure or the laws of the country in which the foreign person is found, and—

(A) the foreign person commits an offense under subsection (a) involving a financial transaction that occurs in whole or in part in the United States;

(B) the foreign person converts, to his or her own use, property in which the United States has an ownership interest by virtue of the entry of an order of forfeiture by a court of the United States; or

(C) the foreign person is a financial institution that maintains a bank account at a financial institution in the United States.

The Financial Crimes Enforcement Network states that digital currencies, which it refers to as convertible virtual currencies (CVCs), continue to be exploited for money laundering in order to evade sanctions or to promote criminal enterprises, particularly online. Virtual currencies are growing as an alternative to traditional payment and money transmission systems (FinCEN, 2019). The agency warned in 2019 that new virtual currencies "appear to be designed with the express purpose of circumventing anti–money laundering/countering the financing of terrorism (AML/CFT) controls" (FinCEN, 2019, p. 2). This makes it harder for law enforcement and security agencies to investigate and prosecute money laundering, terrorist financing, and other financial crimes.

REFERENCES

Albanese, J. (2011). *Transnational Crime and the 21st Century: Criminal Enterprise, Corruption, and Opportunity.* New York: Oxford University Press.
Defendant's Sentencing Submission. (2016). United States v. Budovsky, 13-cr-00368. S. Dist. New York. April 22.

DOJ OPA. (2014). "Liberty Reserve Founder Extradited from Spain." United States Department of Justice, Office of Public Affairs. October 10. https://www.justice .gov/opa/pr/liberty-reserve-founder-extradited-spain.

Economist. (2018). "Digital Detergent: Crypto Money-Laundering." April 26.

FinCEN. (2013). "Guidance [re:] Application of FinCEN's Regulations to Persons Administering, Exchanging or Using Virtual Currencies." US Department of the Treasury, Financial Crimes Enforcement Network. March 18. https://www .fincen.gov/sites/default/files/shared/FIN-2013-G001.pdf.

FinCEN. (2019). "Advisory on Illicit Involving Convertible Virtual Currency." US Department of the Treasury, Financial Crimes Enforcement Network. May 9. https://www.fincen.gov/sites/default/files/advisory/2019-05-10/FinCEN%20 Advisory%20CVC%20FINAL%20508.pdf.

Government's Sentencing Submission. (2016). United States v. Budovsky, 13-cr-00368. S. Dist. New York. May 6.

Indictment. (2013). United States v. Liberty Reserve, et al., 13-cr-00368. S. Dist. New York. May 23.

Opinion and Order. (2019). Budovsky v. United States, 18-cv-7514. S. Dist. New York. August 22.

Richet, J. (2013). "Laundering Money Online: A Review of Cybercriminals Methods." United Nations Office on Drugs and Crime (UNODC). Tools and Resources for Anti-corruption Knowledge. June 1.

Transcript, Arraignment. (2014). United States v. Budovsky, 13-cr-00368. S. Dist. New York. October 14.

Transcript, Sentencing Hearing. (2016). United States v. Budovsky, 13-cr-00368. S. Dist. New York. May 6.

UNODC. (2019). "Money Laundering and Globalization." United Nations Office on Drugs and Crime. https://www.unodc.org/unodc/en/money-laundering /globalization.html.

Zetter, K. (2013). "Liberty Reserve Founder Indicted on $6 Billion Money-Laundering Charges." *Wired*, May 28. https://www.wired.com/2013/05/liberty-reserve-indicted/.

EIGHT

Environmental Crimes

UNITED STATES V. FINCHER, ET AL.

IN 1970 PRESIDENT RICHARD NIXON signed legislation creating the Environmental Protection Agency (EPA), whose purpose, he explained, was to establish and enforce environmental protection standards, conduct research on the adverse effects of pollution and on methods for controlling it, provide grants and other federal assistance to prevent pollution of the environment, and assist in developing policy that protects the environment. The EPA has grown and changed in many ways since then, but is still the chief enforcer of criminal and civil environmental laws. It works with other agencies, both federal and state, to investigate violations of a vast array of regulations and statutes, such as the Clean Water Act, the Resource Conservation and Recovery Act (RCRA), and laws barring the discharge of waste and pollutants, improper disposal of hazardous materials, and importation of certain harmful chemicals, among other environmental hazards.

The consequences of environmental crimes are acute and diffuse. Pollution of air, water, and land can go undetected and still have devastating long-term effects. As an example, the World Health Organization estimates that an estimated 4.2 million deaths each year are the result of exposure to ambient outdoor air pollution (WHO, 2018).

Illegal dumping, destruction of property or wildlife, unlawful emissions, improper disposal of hazardous waste—all of these environmental crimes become white-collar crimes, as well, when committed in the course of an occupation.

The taxonomy developed by Michael M. O'Hear (2004) details the harms that can arise from environmental crimes: (1) immediate physical injury from exposure to harmful products; (2) future physical injuries; (3) emotional distress; (4) disrupted social and economic activities; (5) remediation costs;

(6) property damage; and (7) ecological damage. These can be grouped into three general categories of cost: physical, economic, and community.

The following case study looks at the fallout from an explosion at a munitions storage facility in Camp Minden, Louisiana. The blast shook the surrounding area, and then reverberated through multiple court systems as authorities attempted to parse blame, residents sought peace of mind, and the EPA and the US Army worked to clean up the site. As you read about the case, think about how all the categories of harm listed above are reflected in the case of *United States v. Fincher, et al.* and the related civil cases.

THE BLAST

The explosion happened just before midnight on October 15, 2012, and it lit up the night sky in Webster Parish, Louisiana. The shockwaves shattered windows within a four-mile radius and derailed a nearby freight train, knocking eleven cars off the track. The concussion was felt thirty-five miles away. A 7,200-foot plume of smoke was captured by the National Weather Service's radar (EPA, 2014).

Ground zero was a storage igloo at Camp Minden, Louisiana, a 15,000-acre former military munitions plant used by defense contractors that specialized in disassembling explosives for the army. The storage unit, also called a bunker, was leased by Explo Systems, Inc., which had an $8.6 million contract to demilitarize bombs and resell the recovered materials to mining operations. Investigators would later estimate that the bunker held 124,190 pounds of smokeless powder and that a trailer nearby contained 42,200 pounds of demilitarized M6 propellant. M6 propellant is largely composed of nitrocellulose, a flammable solid. It burns at over 5,000 degrees Fahrenheit, and as it deteriorates, the risk of explosion increases (EPA, n.d.).

Louisiana State Police, the first responders to the scene, investigated the explosion. Despite the magnitude of the blast, there were no injuries or deaths. But the property damage at Camp Minden was considerable—with a destruction and contamination zone of about 1,250-square feet (Indictment, 2016). In all, the state police discovered approximately 6 million pounds of unsecured M6 propellant stored haphazardly, including the 42,200 pounds involved in the blast. The explosive materials should have been stored in certified magazines, commonly called bunkers, but boxes of the M6 were found stacked in buildings, packed into corridors, and stashed among trees outside the buildings. Some of the containers had spilled open (Mohr, 2012). Fearing that ignition of any of the material could trigger a massive chain reaction that could blow up multiple buildings, authorities ordered an evacuation of Doyline, Louisiana (OIG, USDOT, 2018). The town's eight hundred residents were put under a voluntary evacuation order for a week until enough of the M6 could be safely transferred.

A criminal investigation was launched, and a search warrant executed at the facility also turned up approximately 100,000 pounds of TNT-contaminated materials, along with more than 2,700 pounds of contaminated wastewater known as red/pink water, stored in an unsecured warehouse.

REGULATION OF EXPLO SYSTEMS, INC.

Owned by David Fincher and David Smith, Explo Systems had dozens of employees. The company had leased office space, commercial facilities, and munitions storage at Camp Minden since 2002. In 2010, Explo was awarded a contract with the Joint Munitions Command (JMC), a department within the US Army, for the demilitarization of 450,000 155mm artillery propelling charges. The company would be paid $2.9 million, with options to renew the contract in future years. In 2012, JMC agreed to pay Explo $8.6 million to demilitarize 1.3 million propelling charges.

The company also made money by selling the reactive materials it removed from the munitions to mining companies. Ownership of the recovered materials and components transferred to Expo once the company received a certificate of destruction (COD), confirming that the propelling charges had been properly "demilitarized"—defined as "removing the military offensive of defensive advantages of ammunition and explosives" (Indictment, 2016, p. 6). Explo was then entitled to sell the recovered materials to approved, licensed purchasers. The sale of repurposed M6 required an end use certification (EUC), which attests that the buyer agrees to abide by all federal and state laws and local ordinances that apply to handling, storage, and transportation of the explosives and to the resale or export of the materials. The EUC records the identity of the buyer, date of sale, and quantity of M6 being sold. The JMC contract with Explo required that the M6 be disposed of within twelve months of the completed demilitarization (Indictment, 2016).

The handling and dismantling of bombs and explosive materials is highly regulated, both through the Department of Defense contract terms and through federal and state agencies. The Bureau of Alcohol, Tobacco, Firearms, and Explosives enforces laws and regulations concerning the commercial possession and storage of explosives. The Occupational Safety and Health Administration (OSHA) regulates workplace environments to ensure worker safety. The EPA, working with the Louisiana Department of Environmental Quality, enforces federal and state laws, regulations, and rules concerning the treatment, storage, transportation, and disposal of hazardous waste.

To save costs, in 2011 and 2012, Explo did not ship any hazardous waste to permitted waste facilities for treatment and disposal. Instead, the company shipped "reactive" hazardous waste to landfills that were not permitted to take explosive materials. Reactive waste is defined under the RCRA as that which "readily explodes or undergoes violent reactions," such as discarded munitions and explosives (Indictment, 2016, p. 11). Paperwork submitted to those nonhazardous waste landfills in Arkansas and Louisiana omitted mention that the shipment contained TNT. But shipping the waste made room for new shipments of M6 propellants to arrive for processing.

In early 2012, Explo officials asked to lease additional space, but the request was denied because the company was roughly $400,000 behind on its rent, according to the Louisiana National Guard. The company worked out a payment plan on the rent owed, but did not bring up the need for more space again (Mohr, 2012).

Following the blast, Explo employees worked with the Louisiana State Police to clean up the site to mitigate the risk to public safety posed by the improper storage. In May 2013, the state police declared that sufficient explosives had been moved to proper locations, with more than 10 million pounds of explosive M6 propellant, 100,000 pounds of flammable solid materials, and 130,000 pounds of Tritonal transported to new storage areas (Louisiana State Police, 2013). As it made the announcement about the public safety risk, the state police also announced that it had revoked Explo's license to handle explosives, pending the outcome of all civil and criminal investigations. But within weeks the company had its licenses reinstated after a judge issued a temporary restraining order in Explo's favor (Roy, 2013). The judge ruled that Explo could continue to operate, but only in regard to its efforts to market and sell the product already there and not to produce more (KSLA Staff, 2013).

Just two weeks later, however, six Explo Systems employees were arrested on state charges of mishandling explosives. The indictment named three executives—Explo Systems president David Fincher and Vice Presidents David Smith and William Terry Wright. Also arrested were Lionel Koons, an inventory control manager, and two lower-level employees—a plant manager and quality service manager. A seventh employee was added to the case a year later. The company was also indicted.

The felony charges included unlawful storage of explosives, reckless use of explosives, failure to obtain a magazine license, failure to properly mark explosive materials, and failure to keep accurate inventory, as well as conspiracy to commit the substantive charges (Amy, 2013). If convicted, the men faced sentences between 2 and 10 years in prison. All of the defendants pleaded not guilty, but three later changed their pleas and agreed to testify against the owners (Roy, 2013). One defendant told the court that he had warned his supervisors that the explosive product was backlogged but his warnings had been ignored. Another defendant, inventory manager Lionel Koons, said he had asked to stop new incoming deliveries when there was no room to store the product, but he had been overruled by the company's owners and managers. Under the plea agreement, the men were sentenced to 90 days in jail, which was suspended, and fined $1,000.

BANKRUPTCY AND CIVIL CASES

In August 2013, Explo Systems, Inc., filed for bankruptcy. The remaining materials it owned and possessed at Camp Minden were "abandoned," according to the EPA (EPA, 2014). This left a looming question about who would pay to clean up what US Attorney David C. Joseph called "the largest illegal dumping ground of military explosives in the history of the United States" (USAO-WDLa, 2018). The dispute centered on the EPA and the army.

The EPA issued an RCRA endangerment order against the army requiring it to conduct the cleanup at Camp Minden, estimated to cost about $38 million. The order, issued under RCRA section 7003, found that the army contributed to the illegal storage and handling, and said that storage of the unstable materials created a risk that the propellant would autoignite, which posed an "imminent and substantial endangerment to public health and the environment" (Unilateral Administrative Order, 2014). The army objected to the EPA's order, claiming that the federal agency did not have such authority over other federal agencies. In addition, the army argued that it wasn't responsible for cleaning up a site owned by a contractor. Roughly two years after the explosion, US senator Mary Landrieu announced a negotiated settlement according to which the United States would pick up the cost and the Louisiana Military Department, which owned and operated Camp Minden, would oversee the cleanup efforts. Under the agreement, the EPA withdrew the endangerment order.

That still left approximately 16 million pounds of dangerous material to dispose of, and local residents were concerned about an open-burn process that had been proposed. Officials said the process would take about a year to complete and would cost nearly $20 million (EPA, n.d.). But local opposition to that plan grew because it would require burning 80,000 pounds of the propellant every day for two hundred days, which a grassroots organization said would be an environmental disaster (Robertson, 2015). The EPA put the plan on hold in 2014 to work with local authorities and the community in exploring alternative methods.

Eventually, the Louisiana National Guard hired a contractor to design a burn chamber that would capture any pollution. In 2017, the Guard announced that all of the unstable materials at Camp Minden had been burned (AP, 2017).

FEDERAL CRIMINAL CHARGES

As cleanup efforts continued at the site, a federal investigation continued in the background, led by the EPA Criminal Investigation Division in coordination with the US Army Criminal Investigation, the Department of Defense Criminal Investigative Service, the FBI, the Office of Inspector General of the US Department of Transportation, Louisiana State Police, and the Webster Parish Sheriff's Office. The state felony charges were still pending for four of the defendants originally charged.

In August 2016, a federal grand jury handed up an indictment for six Explo Systems executives and employees (Indictment, 2016). The thirty-two-count indictment charged David Fincher, David Smith, William Terry Wright, Lionel Koons, Kenneth Lampkin, and Charles Callihan with conspiracy, making false statements, and wire fraud. All of the defendants were charged in the conspiracy count, which alleged that they concealed or obstructed oversight agencies by hiding the storage and handling conditions of the M6 propellant and reactive hazardous waste at Explo.

The government alleged that Fincher, Smith, Wright, Koons, and Lampkin submitted false, forged, or fabricated end user certifications to the Joint Munitions Command that purported to show demilitarized M6 propellant had been sold, when it had not. Other alleged false statements included omitting material information about the presence of reactive materials in shipments sent to nonhazardous waste landfills in Louisiana and Arkansas, which made room for the storage of new shipments of M6 propellant. Those five defendants were also named in six wire fraud counts (18 U.S.C. § 1343) for purportedly submitting false proofs of sale and EUCs for M6 propellant to trigger payments from JMC to Explo.

Callihan was charged with one count of making a false statement for allegedly lying to an OSHA agent about whether the propellant was stored only in approved magazines. And Koons was charged with falsely telling a JMC official to cease deliveries of propellant to Explo because the company was in the middle of an audit, when the real reason was that the Louisiana State Police were executing a search warrant at the Camp Minden facility and had ordered the company to stop accepting deliveries because there was insufficient storage.

The EPA Criminal Investigation Division executed a search warrant in January 2013, seizing computers and documents. Its officials also conducted extensive interviews with employees and vendors associated with Explo, and conducted scientific testing at the facility (Sentencing Hearing Transcript, November 28, 2018). Vice-president and co-owner of Explo Systems, Inc., David Smith pleaded guilty to two counts, conspiracy and making false statements, in a cooperation agreement with the government. Lionel Koons and Kenneth Lampkin also pleaded guilty and agreed to cooperate with the government.

The three remaining defendants, Fincher, Wright, and Callihan, elected to go to trial in June 2018. But days before the trial was to start, Explo Systems president and co-owner David Fincher died. Wright and Callihan changed their pleas to guilty.

At the conclusion of a two-day sentencing hearing, Judge Elizabeth E. Foote imposed sentences ranging from 2 to 5 years. David Smith told the court, "I made a grave error in judgment and wish that I could turn back the clock and make drastically different decisions, but I can't. And the decisions

I did make have cost me my career, my professional reputation, and any hope of providing for my family in the future" (Sentencing Hearing Transcript, November 29, 2018, p. 307).

The judge noted that aggravating factors in Smith's sentence were the loss amount—an estimated $34 million in damages that the US government paid to repair and clean up the Explo site; the high risk of death or serious bodily injury involved in the offense; and the supervisor's role he had in the offense as an owner of the company. Because Smith pleaded guilty early and cooperated with the government, the judge departed downward from the advisory sentence of 5 years, imposing a sentence of 55 months.

In crafting the sentencing, Judge Foote said that she wanted the punishment to reflect the defendant's culpability in relation to the others' and the nature of the offense. "This was not an offense that occurred once,' she said; "in actuality it occurred daily over a long period of time" (Sentencing Hearing Transcript, November 29, 2018, p. 312). Smith's attorney said that the Webster Parish district attorney agreed to run any sentence in his state case concurrent with the federal sentence so that Smith would not serve any additional time.

Lampkin pleaded guilty to one count of making a false statement. As the program manager for the army contract, he was responsible for ensuring compliance with the contract's terms. In his plea agreement, he admitted that he intentionally submitted false EUCs to show that Explo was selling the materials, and that he helped to conceal the improper storage conditions (Sentencing Hearing Transcript, November 29, 2018). Though the advisory sentencing range under the guideline was 60 months, the statutory maximum sentence, the judge took into account that Lampkin had lower relative culpability than the others in the case and sentenced him to 45 months in prison.

Wright, the former vice president of operations, had been responsible for the company's day-to-day operations. He was the last defendant to plead guilty, the day prior to the start of the scheduled trial. The court sentenced Wright to the maximum statutory sentence of 5 years, reflecting his relative culpability in the offense.

Lionel Koons pleaded guilty to making false statements in violation of 18 U.S.C. § 1001. As the traffic and inventory control manager, he had overseen the receipt of the bombs and the artillery propelling charges, the shipment of recovered materials, and the movement of materials between the Explo facilities within Camp Minden. He pleaded guilty to sending false information to JMC during the execution of the search warrant by Louisiana States Police.

42 U.S.C. § 6928(d)

(d) Criminal penalties

Any person who—

(1) knowingly transports or causes to be transported any hazardous waste identified or listed under this subchapter to a facility which does not have a permit under this subchapter, or pursuant to title I of the Marine Protection, Research, and Sanctuaries Act (86 Stat. 1052) [33 U.S.C. 1411 et seq.],

(2) knowingly treats, stores, or disposes of any hazardous waste identified or listed under this subchapter—
   (A) without a permit under this subchapter or pursuant to title I of the Marine Protection, Research, and Sanctuaries Act (86 Stat. 1052) [33 U.S.C. 1411 et seq.]; or
   (B) in knowing violation of any material condition or require-ment of such permit; or
   (C) in knowing violation of any material condition or requirement of any applicable interim status regulations or standards;

(3) knowingly omits material information or makes any false material statement or representation in any application, label, manifest, record, report, permit, or other document filed, maintained, or used for purposes of compliance with regulations promulgated by the Administrator (or by a State in the case of an authorized State program) under this subchapter;

(4) knowingly generates, stores, treats, transports, disposes of, exports, or otherwise handles any hazardous waste or any used oil not identified or listed as a hazardous waste under this subchapter . . . and who knowingly destroys, alters, conceals, or fails to file any record, application, manifest, report, or other document required to be maintained or filed for purposes of compliance with regulations promulgated by the Administrator (or by a State in the case of an authorized State program) under this subchapter;

(5) knowingly transports without a manifest, or causes to be transported without a manifest, any hazardous waste or any used oil not identified or listed as a hazardous waste under this subchapter required by regulations promulgated under this

subchapter (or by a State in the case of a State program authorized under this subchapter) to be accompanied by a manifest;

(6) knowingly exports a hazardous waste identified or listed under
this subchapter (A) without the consent of the receiving country
or, (B) where there exists an international agreement between
the United States and the government of the receiving country
establishing notice, export, and enforcement procedures for the
transportation, treatment, storage, and disposal of hazardous
wastes, in a manner which is not in conformance with such
agreement; or

(7) knowingly stores, treats, transports, or causes to be transported,
disposes of, or otherwise handles any used oil not identified or
listed as a hazardous waste under this subchapter—
    (A) in knowing violation of any material condition or require-
ment of a permit under this subchapter; or
    (B) in knowing violation of any material condition or require-
ment of any applicable regulations or standards under this
chapter;

shall, upon conviction, be subject to a fine of not more than
$50,000 for each day of violation, or imprisonment not to exceed
two years (five years in the case of a violation of paragraph (1)
or (2)), or both. If the conviction is for a violation committed
after a first conviction of such person under this paragraph, the
maximum punishment under the respective paragraph shall be
doubled with respect to both fine and imprisonment.

A. M. Stroud, Koons's attorney, said his client "stands in a little different
position from the others. He had the misfortune of being prosecuted twice.
He was prosecuted in state court and entered a plea of guilty, served his probation without incident.... Mr. Koons thought he was through, and years
later, the government came in and charged him again.... I acknowledge that
under the law, it's not double jeopardy, but it was still a bomb dropped on
Mr. Koons when he thought he had served his sentence" (Sentencing Hearing
Transcript, November 29, 2018, p. 390). Taking his lower level of culpability
into account, the judge imposed a sentence of 41 months in prison.

Charles Callihan pleaded guilty to a violation of 42 U.S.C. § 6928(d)(3) for
knowingly omitting material information in EPA compliance documents—

specifically, for withholding from the landfill's managers knowledge that the shipments from Explo contained TNT. He was sentenced to the maximum statutory penalty under that statute, 2 years in prison.

All of the men had led exemplary lives, and that made imposing prison sentences even more difficult, the judge said. But she had to balance that fact with the harm and the extreme risk that they had caused to the community and other workers at Camp Minden.

The restitution order for Smith, Explo System's co-owner, amounted to more than $35 million—the cost to clean and repair the blast site. But the rest of the employees indicted, who had not profited from their false statements with profit sharing or bonuses, were ordered to pay restitution in an amount equal to the salary that they had received during the period the criminal conduct was ongoing. The amounts ranged from $149,000 to $207,000.

POSTSCRIPT

As a result of the Camp Minden explosion, the Louisiana legislature approved a law expanding the authority of the state police to inspect and regulate businesses handling explosives. It was sent to Governor Bobby Jindal's desk, but was not signed.

REFERENCES

Amy, J. (2013). "6 Arrested in Camp Minden Explosives Investigation." Fox 8 Local First, June 19. https://www.fox8live.com/story/22637088/la-company-managers-indicted-in-explosives-case/.

AP. (2017). "All Unstable Artillery Propellant at Camp Minden Burned." Associated Press, April 22. https://www.armytimes.com/news/your-army/2017/04/22/all-unstable-artillery-propellant-at-camp-minden-burned/.

Emerson, S. (2018). *Vice Magazine*, November 30. "Five Men Responsible for 7,200-foot Mushroom Cloud Explosion in Louisiana Sentenced to Prison." https://www.vice.com/en_us/article/8xpmv4/five-men-responsible-for-7200-foot-mushroom-cloud-explosion-in-louisiana-sentenced-to-prison-camp-minden.

EPA. (2014). "Explo Systems, Inc., Site Removal Action: Camp Minden, Webster Parish, Louisiana." Environmental Protection Agency. (April). https://www.epa.gov/la/camp-minden-fact-sheet-april-2014.

EPA. (2018). "EPA and Law Enforcement Partners Announce Sentencing in Louisiana Explosive Waste Disposal Case." Environmental Protection Agency. November 29.

Accessed September 29, 2019. https://www.epa.gov/newsreleases/epa-and-law-enforcement-partners-announce-sentencing-louisiana-explosive-waste-disposal.

EPA. n.d. "Camp Minden Questions and Answers." Environmental Protection Agency. Accessed September 29, 2019. https://www.epa.gov/la/camp-minden-questions-and-answers.

KSLA Staff. (2013). "Explo Employees Facing Felony Charges Plead Not Guilty; Trial Date Set." KSLA News 12, July 29. https://www.ksla.com/story/22957208/explo-employees-facing-felony-charges-plead-not-guilty-trial-date-set/

Louisiana State Police. (2013). "Camp Minden Update: All Explosives Now Properly Stored and Explo Licenses Revoked." (May 20.) http://lsp.org/news.html.

Mohr, H. (2012). "Explo Faced Scrutiny before La. Scare." *Washington Examiner,* December 11. https://www.washingtonexaminer.com/apnewsbreak-explo-faced-scrutiny-before-la-scare.

O'Hear, M.M. (2004). "Sentencing the Green-Collar Offender: Punishment, Culpability, and Environmental Crime." *Journal of Criminal Law and Criminology* 95(1), 133–276.

OIG, USDOT (2018). "Louisiana Company Employee Pleads Guilty to False Statements Related to Improper Disposal of Ammunitions." Office of Inspector General, US Department of Transportation. April 24. https://www.oig.dot.gov/library-item/36531.

Robertson, C. (2015). "Louisiana Parish Fights Plan to Burn Tons of Propellant No One Wants." *New York Times,* March 18. https://www.nytimes.com/2015/03/19/us/louisiana-parish-fights-plan-to-burn-tons-of-propellant-no-one-wants.html.

Roy, C. (2013). "Explo Gets Licenses Revoked by LSP Back, at Least Temporarily." KSLA News 12, June 11. https://www.ksla.com/story/22564307/explo-gets-licenses-revoked-by-lsp-back-at-least-temporarily/.

USAO-WDLa. (2018). "Explo Officials Sentenced for Roles in Conspiracy That Led to Illegal Dumping of Munitions and Explosion at Camp Minden." Department of Justice, US Attorney's Office, Western District Louisiana. November 29. https://www.justice.gov/usao-wdla/pr/explo-officials-sentenced-roles-conspiracy-led-illegal-dumping-munitions-and-explosion.

Wellborn, V. (2015). "Camp Minden Tenants to Practice Safety Plan." Shreveport Times. (January 17). https://www.thetowntalk.com/story/news/2015/01/17/camp-minden-tenants-practice-safety-plan/21927725/.

WHO. (2018). "Ambient Air Pollution—A Major Threat to Health and Climate." World Health Organization. Accessed August 8, 2020. https://www.who.int/airpollution/ambient/en/.

Court Documents

Indictment. (2016). United States v. Fincher, 16-cr-00214, W. Dist. Louisiana. August 25.

Sentencing Hearing Transcript. (November 28, 2018) United States v. Fincher, 16-cr-00214, W. Dist. Louisiana.

Sentencing Hearing Transcript. (November 29, 2018). United States v. Fincher, 16-cr-00214, W. Dist. Louisiana.

Unilateral Administrative Order. (2014). In the Matter of The United States Department of the Army. RCRA-06-2014-0902. United States Environmental Protection Agency, Region 6, Dallas, Texas. March 18.

NINE

Foreign Corrupt Practices Act

UNITED STATES V. AVON PRODUCTS, INC., AVON PRODUCTS (CHINA) CO., LTD.

SINCE 1977, IT'S BEEN ILLEGAL for United States business interests to bribe foreign officials. The Foreign Corrupt Practices Act (FCPA) came about after Congress learned that defense contractors and oil companies maintained "slush funds" on their books to pay government officials in foreign countries in order to gain business advantages (*United States v. Kay*, 359 F.3d 738 [5th Cir. 2004]). The FCPA prohibits bribery that encourages officials to misuse their discretionary authority or that disrupts market efficiency and US foreign relations.

Cases investigated and settled by US agencies in the past five years included such conduct as a company's executive board paying millions of dollars to politicians and political parties to stop a parliamentary inquiry into the company's contracts (DOJ OPA, September 27, 2018); a company using a Libyan broker to pay bribes related to investments made by a state-owned financial institution (DOJ OPA, June 4, 2018); and a corporation retaining a key official of a state-owned airline as a consultant for $875,000 in return for "little work" while negotiating a valuable contract with that airline (SEC, 2018). In each of those cases, the companies sought an advantage with government officials that would benefit their business position—a favor granted or a gift offered in return for preferential treatment. The conduct covered by the FCPA may involve large sums of money, both in the bribes paid and in the resulting fines. The US Securities and Exchange Commission (SEC) and the US Department of Justice also pursue seemingly smaller violations—such as the practices seen in this case, where company officials wined and dined government officials and gave improper gifts of designer handbags and personal travel.

The FCPA applies to three categories of people and businesses. First, it covers "issuers." An issuer is any entity whose securities are registered in the United States or that is required to file periodic reports with the SEC, as well as "any officer, director, employee, or agent of such issuer or any stockholder thereof acting on behalf of such issuer" (15 U.S.C. § 78dd-1). This includes corporate entities that aren't US companies and individuals who aren't residents of the United States. Second, the antibribery statute covers "domestic concerns," which refers to a person who is a citizen, national, or resident of the United States, or any business entity that has its principal place of business in the United States (15 U.S.C. § 78dd-2). This includes officers, directors, employees, or agents of those companies, or a stockholder acting on behalf of the business.

Third, the law covers foreign nationals or businesses, or agents of these, who are neither issuers nor domestic concerns but who act to further an illicit bribe on US territory (15 U.S.C. § 78dd-3). This section was added in 1998 to conform to the antibribery conventions adopted by the Organization for Economic Cooperation and Development (OECD) in a collaborative effort between forty-three countries to promote strong and fair economies.

To prove a violation of the FCPA, the government must show that a person or business covered by one of the above sections made a payment offer, authorized a payment, or promised to pay money or give something of value, either directly or indirectly, to certain recipients, such as a foreign official, foreign political party, or candidate for foreign political office, or to an intermediary expected to pass the funds or gifts to such an individual. The money or gift must be offered "corruptly," that is, for the purpose of influencing an official act in a way that would violate the official's lawful duty, securing an improper advantage, or inducing the individual to use their influence with a foreign government to alter a government act. The purpose of that corrupt act must be to help the company to obtain or retain business.

Most important, the government has the burden to prove the corrupt intent of the bribery scheme. The Eighth Circuit US Court of Appeals, in *United States v. Liebo* (923 F.2d 1308 [8th Cir. 1991]), upheld a jury instruction that defined *corruptly* in the following way: "The offer, promise to pay, payment or authorization of payment, must be intended to induce the recipient to misuse his official position or to influence someone else to do so. . . . [A]n act is 'corruptly' done if done 'voluntarily [a]nd intentionally, and with a bad purpose of accomplishing either an unlawful end or result, or a lawful end or result by some unlawful method or means'" (923 F.2d at 1312).

The FCPA can be enforced in a civil suit in which the SEC investigates and resolves cases with fines and disgorgement. Companies and individuals can also be prosecuted criminally by the US Department of Justice. In order for the bribe to result in a criminal sentence, the government must show the act was undertaken willfully—and "willful blindness" is not a defense to the statute that bars payments made to an intermediary. Willful blindness is defined as a person's state of mind: "when knowledge of the existence of a particular circumstance is required for an offense, such knowledge is established if a person is aware of a high probability of the existence of such circumstance, unless the person actually believes that such circumstance does not exist" (15 U.S.C. § 78dd-1(F)(2)).

The FCPA also mandates internal controls and record keeping on the part of issuers, though not domestic concerns or other persons. These accounting provisions fall within the civil enforcement authority of the SEC, though the Justice Department can bring criminal charges if it can prove that the defendant willfully circumvented or failed to implement a system of internal accounting controls or willfully falsified books and records (O'Sullivan, 2012, p. 584). Policing internal books and records and monitoring the practices of overseas arms of US corporations and issuers are difficult, so the FCPA provides for mitigation of a sentence if the corporation self-reports. Companies that report their violations can expect more lenient treatment. The Department of Justice and the SEC also rely on tips, especially from whistleblowers.

Corruption in the business community has direct and indirect effects on taxpayers, citizens, and legitimate companies (Albanese, 2011). A corrupt relationship between a government and a private business can increase costs to consumers, cause the misuse of taxpayer resources, and undermine public trust in government. Business officials who want to play by the rules get penalized, which damages economic development.

In the case study examined in this chapter, a trusted name in American business turned itself in to the SEC for its conduct as it entered a developing direct-selling industry market in China. As you read this chapter, think about how companies can best determine where the line is between a gift that shows respect to an official and their culture's tradition, and one motivated by the "corrupt" intent barred by the FCPA.

Excerpt of Remarks by Deputy Attorney General Rod Rosenstein

34th International Conference on the Foreign Corrupt Practices Act, November 29, 2017

There was a time in the 1960s and '70s when paying bribes was viewed as a necessary part of doing business abroad. Some American companies were unapologetic about making corrupt payments. Corruption was rife in many parts of the world. There were European countries that allowed companies to deduct bribes on their corporate tax returns, as business expenses.

In 1976, the U.S. Senate Banking Committee revealed that hundreds of U.S. companies had made corrupt foreign payments. The payments totaled hundreds of millions of dollars. The Committee concluded that there was a need for anti-bribery legislation. Its report reasoned that "[c]orporate bribery is bad business" and "fundamentally destructive" in a free market society.

Paying bribes may still be common in some places. But that does not make it right. As Thomas Jefferson famously said: "On matters of style, swim with the current. On matters of principle, stand like a rock." . . .

One of the lessons I learned in business school is that ethical conduct is a good investment. Companies sometimes gain a short-term advantage over competitors by cutting corners, but in the long run, companies with a culture of integrity usually prevail in the marketplace. Good people want to work for honest businesses. Investors trust them. Customers like to do business with them. . . .

The United States plays a central role in the worldwide fight against corruption, and we serve as a role model. Following our lead, many other countries have joined America by implementing their own anti-corruption laws. Those laws do not just encourage good business. They promote good government.

The Organization for Economic Cooperation and Development adopted an Anti-Bribery Convention in 1997. That convention fuels the growing international rejection of corruption. Forty-three nations participate in the OECD Anti-Bribery Convention. The agreement establishes legally binding standards. Member countries are required to adopt laws that criminalize bribery of foreign public officials in international business transactions. Just a few months ago, a new country, Costa Rica, ratified the convention. These 43 nations recognize the importance of a level playing field that protects citizens and honest businesses.

Earlier this year, Attorney General Sessions spoke about the harmful consequences of corruption. It leads to increased prices, substandard products and services, and reduced investment. It is no coincidence that crime syndicates and authoritarian rulers use corruption to enrich themselves. They engage in corruption to consolidate political power and defeat legitimate political adversaries. . . .

Effective deterrence of corporate corruption requires prosecution of culpable individuals. We should not just announce large corporate fines and celebrate penalizing shareholders.

Most American companies are serious about engaging in lawful business practices. Those companies want to do the right thing. They need our support to protect them from criminals who seek unfair advantages.

Law enforcement agencies prosecute criminal wrongdoing only after it occurs. Those prosecutions achieve deterrence indirectly. But a company with a robust compliance program can prevent corruption and reduce the need for enforcement.

That frees agents and prosecutors to focus on people who are committing other financial crimes. It also allows them to focus on different threats to the American people, including terrorism, gang violence, drug trafficking, child exploitation, and human smuggling. People who commit those horrendous crimes do not make voluntary disclosures.

Threats to American safety and security will grow more complex over time. We need corporate America to help us detect and fight those threats.

As Attorney General Jeff Sessions explained, "Societies where the rule of law is treasured . . . tend to flourish and succeed. Societies where the rule of law is subject to political whims and personal biases tend to become . . . afflicted by corruption, poverty, and human suffering."

The most fundamental mission of the Department of Justice is to protect the American people by enforcing the rule of law.

The rule of law is good for business. It allows businesses to compete for work, enter contracts, make investments, and project revenue with some assurance about the future. It establishes a mechanism to resolve disputes, and it provides a degree of protection from arbitrary government action.

Corporate America should regard law enforcement as an ally. We support the rule of law, which establishes and safeguards a vibrant economic marketplace for your products and services.

The government should provide incentives for companies to engage in ethical corporate behavior. That means fully cooperating with government investigations, and doing what is necessary to remediate misconduct—including implementing a robust compliance program. Good corporate behavior also means notifying law enforcement about wrongdoing.

The incentive system set forth in the Department's FCPA Pilot Program motivates and rewards companies that want to do the right thing and voluntarily disclose misconduct. In the first year of the Pilot Program, the FCPA Unit received 22 voluntary disclosures, compared to 13 during the previous year. In total, during the year and a half that the Pilot Program was in effect, the FCPA Unit received 30 voluntary disclosures, compared to 18 during the previous 18-month period.

We analyzed the Pilot Program and concluded that it proved to be a step forward in fighting corporate crime. We also determined that there were opportunities for improvement.

So today, I am announcing a revised FCPA Corporate Enforcement Policy.

The new policy enables the Department to efficiently identify and punish criminal conduct, and it provides guidance and greater certainty for companies struggling with the question of whether to make voluntary disclosures of wrongdoing. . . .

We expect the new policy to reassure corporations that want to do the right thing. It will increase the volume of voluntary disclosures, and enhance our ability to identify and punish culpable individuals. The new policy, like the rest of the Department's internal operating policies, creates no private rights and is not enforceable in court. But it does promote consistency by attorneys throughout the Department. Establishing internal policies helps guide our exercise of discretion and combat the perception that prosecutors act in an arbitrary manner.

The new policy does not provide a guarantee. We cannot eliminate all uncertainty. Preserving a measure of prosecutorial discretion is central to ensuring the exercise of justice. But with this new policy, we strike the balance in favor of greater clarity about our decision-making process.

The advantage of the policy for businesses is to provide transparency about the benefits available if they satisfy the requirements. We want corporate officers and board members to better understand the costs and benefits of cooperation. The policy therefore specifies what we mean by voluntary disclosure, full cooperation, and timely and appropriate remediation.

Even if a company does not make a voluntary disclosure, benefits are still available for cooperation and remediation. Those steps assist the Department in running an efficient investigation that identifies culpable individuals. They also reduce the likelihood that crimes will be committed again.

I want to highlight a few of the policy's enhancements.

First, the FCPA Corporate Enforcement Policy states that when a company satisfies the standards of voluntary self-disclosure, full cooperation, and timely and appropriate remediation, there will be a presumption that the Department will resolve the company's case through a declination.* That presumption may be overcome only if there are aggravating circumstances related to the nature and seriousness of the offense, or if the offender is a criminal recidivist.

It makes sense to treat corporations differently than individuals, because corporate liability is vicarious; it is only derivative of individual liability.

Second, if a company voluntarily discloses wrongdoing and satisfies all other requirements, but aggravating circumstances compel an enforcement action, the Department will recommend a 50% reduction off the low end of the Sentencing Guidelines fine range. . . .

Third, the Policy provides details about how the Department evaluates an appropriate compliance program, which will vary depending on the size and resources of a business.

The Policy therefore specifies some of the hallmarks of an effective compliance and ethics program. Examples include fostering a culture of compliance; dedicating sufficient resources to compliance activities; and ensuring that experienced compliance personnel have appropriate access to management and to the board.

We expect that these adjustments, along with adding the FCPA Corporate Enforcement Policy to the U.S. Attorneys' Manual, will incentivize responsible corporate behavior and reduce cynicism about enforcement.

Of course, companies are free to choose not to comply with the FCPA Corporate Enforcement Policy. A company needs to adhere to the policy only if it wants the Department's prosecutors to follow the policy's guidelines.

*That is, through declining to prosecute the case.

Companies that violate the FCPA are always free to choose a different path. In those instances, if crimes come to our attention through whistleblowers or other means, the Department will take appropriate action consistent with the facts, the law, and the Principles of Federal Prosecution of Business Organizations. . . .

Allow me to conclude with the observation that corrupt government officials and criminals who bribe them learn from the cases we bring and the investigative techniques we use.

Criminals try to evade law enforcement. But they also need to evade internal controls and compliance programs, if those internal controls and programs exist. Honest companies pose a meaningful deterrent to corruption.

Companies can protect themselves by exercising caution in choosing their business associates and by ensuring appropriate oversight of their activities.

There is an ancient proverb that counsels, "If you want to know a person's character, consider his friends."

My advice is to make sure that you can stand proudly with the company you keep.

Source: Rosenstein, 2017.

THE BOOKS AND RECORDS

Avon is a global beauty products company that sells its cosmetics and skincare products in more than a hundred countries. Those products are sold directly to consumers by salespeople going door to door. Avon is a leader in the world of network marketing, also known as multilevel marketing or direct selling. As many as 6 million active Avon sales representatives are independent contractors who purchase products from Avon at a discount and sell them to their customers (Deferred Prosecution Agreement, 2014). The company also employs as many as 50,000 people globally, approximately 6,000 of whom work in the United States. The company is headquartered and incorporated in New York, and its shares trade on the New York Stock Exchange.

In 1998, the Chinese government outlawed direct selling in China. But in 2001, as a condition of its entry into the World Trade Organization, China agreed to lift that ban. To test its regulations, officials decided to issue one company a temporary license to conduct direct sales. That test license went to Avon China, an indirect subsidiary of Avon that was incorporated in China. Avon China manufactured and sold beauty and health care products through direct sales, as well as through "beauty boutiques," which were independently owned and operated. The test license was issued to Avon China in March 2005 and a year later, the company obtained its national direct-selling license. By July 2006, it had obtained all of the provincial and municipal approvals needed to conduct direct selling.

But even before the corporation received the test license, executives and employees of Avon China had been giving gifts and cash to Chinese government officials. Starting in 2004, Avon China executives and employees provided the government officials with travel, meals, and entertainment (Deferred Prosecution Agreement, 2014). Gifts included Avon products and luxury items such as designer wallets, handbags, and watches. Over four years, the company spent approximately $8 million on government officials, falsifying the transactions on Avon's books and records by describing the expenses as employee related, by misleadingly categorizing or concealing the gifts' nature and purpose (as, for example, employee travel, entertainment samples, or public relations business entertainment), or by using false invoices to a consulting company. Avon China employees would also conceal the recipients' names or the price of the gift(Deferred Prosecution Agreement, 2014).

Examples of the spending and falsified records included:

- Avon China employees spent $890 on gifts for government officials, but described it as entertainment expenses and omitted the recipients' names and the purpose of the gifts from the records.

- In March 2008, an Avon China employee described a $960 Louis Vuitton handbag for a government official as "public relations entertainment" expense.

- An $800 Gucci bag given to a government official was described as "business entertainment" expenses.

- In 2006, Avon China employees described $8,100 spent on meals and entertainment for government officials as "sales-business entertainment."

- In January 2008, executives spent $3,200 on meals, entertainment, and lodging for government officials that was recorded as "business entertainment" and employee "accommodation." The real purpose of the meals and entertainment provided to these officials was to get government approval to sell a product that did not meet government standards.

Avon China also falsified records of paying the costs of personal vacations, sightseeing trips, and a beach holiday for government officials and their families. The company recorded those expenses as "study trips" or "site visits" by government officials (Deferred Prosecution Agreement, 2014, p. A-13). One Avon China–sponsored trip brought to the United States six officials from the Guangdong Food and Drug Administration, the agency responsible for approving Avon China's health care products for sale. The $90,000 excursion was recorded as business-related travel to Avon's research and development facility in upstate New York. But the officials never visited Avon's headquarters in New York, spent one morning at the research and development facility, and used the rest of the eighteen-day trip to sightsee in Vancouver, Montreal, Ottawa, Toronto, Philadelphia, Washington, DC, Seattle, Los Angeles, Las Vegas, and Hawaii.

Other expenses that were falsely recorded included:

- $15,400 paid for a "site visit/inspection" so that government officials could travel to Guangzhou, Shenzhen, and Sanya, though the underlying records included charges for a tour guide, sightseeing bus, and items purchased at a beach.
- $11,000 described as "business entertainment" that was actually a personal trip for two government officials to celebrate the Chinese New Year. One went on a nine-day excursion to Hainan Island, and the other took a twelve-day holiday tour of Hong Kong and Macau.

In August 2006, an Avon China executive approved a request to send approximately $12,000 to a government official's bank account to avoid paying a fine for violating China's direct-selling regulations. To support the request, an employee submitted a handwritten certificate, purportedly from a government agency, that falsely stated the official would give the funds to the government bureau. The money was sent in three separate wires to the government official's personal bank account. On Avon China's books, the cost was reported as legitimate management and government-relations expenses.

Broadly, the purpose of these payments—to obtain and retain business—put them under the FCPA's purview. Specifically, Avon China executives and employees were paying to get favorable judicial treatment, to obtain approval to sell nutritional supplements and health care products that did not yet meet government standards, and to retain their direct-selling licenses. The company also sought to avoid negative media reports; it paid tens of thousands of dollars to suppress an article in a government-owned newspaper that would have said Avon China was improperly recruiting sales associates. The report could have jeopardized the company's direct-selling license. At the request of the government official at the newspaper who would decide whether the article would run, Avon China paid $77,500 to become a "sponsor" of the paper.

The record of suspect payments dated back as early as 2003 when Avon China contracted with a consulting firm to handle crisis management and government relations and to coordinate with public security authorities (Deferred Prosecution Agreement, 2014). Although the company paid between $2,000 and $7,000 a month, plus expenses, Avon China conducted no due diligence regarding the consulting company and did not require the company to comply with Avon's code of conduct. Between October 2003 and September 2008, Avon China executives and employees paid the consulting company additional money for ambiguously described services, even though at least one Avon executive knew the invoices were false and no legitimate services were being provided. For example, Avon China described $43,000 paid to the consulting company as public relations fees and as "sponsorship" of an art exhibit that never occurred.

THE INTERNAL INVESTIGATION

Avon, the parent company, learned that employees and executives of Avon China had routinely provided things of value to Chinese government officials and failed to document it. But instead of ensuring that the practice stopped and the individuals responsible were disciplined, Avon concealed its internal concerns about the accuracy of Avon China's books and records and about its practices of giving gifts to government officials.

A senior manager in Avon's internal audit group reported in June 2005 that Avon China was not maintaining proper records of entertainment for government officials. The auditor reported that an Avon China executive had explained that the practice was intentional, as information regarding entertainment was "quite sensitive" (Deferred Prosecution Agreement, 2014). Avon's internal auditors reviewed travel and entertainment expenses and issued a draft report documenting their conclusion that Avon China's expenses included high-value gifts and meals offered to government officials on an ongoing basis, the majority recorded as expenses relating to gifts, meals, sponsorships, and travel. The purpose of the expenses was to maintain relationships with government officials. The report also noted that a third-party consultant was paid a substantial sum of money to interact with the government, though the services it had provided were vague and unknown. The consultant was not contractually required to follow the FCPA and had not been monitored by Avon China. The draft report also found that the payments and the lack of accurate detailed records may have violated the FCPA or other anticorruption laws.

In response, Avon China executives told the internal audit team that they could not record the names of government officials who were given gifts or who were entertained, because government officials didn't want a paper trail. If the gifts were revealed, the government officials would cut ties with Avon China, which would harm the company's expansion efforts. Avon China's management team objected to the report's mention of the gifts and potential FCPA violations for fear that the report might be seen by government officials in China, other Avon or Avon China employees, or competitors.

Avon executives agreed with Avon China executives to delete any mention of the gifts from the final audit report. An Avon executive directed the internal audit team to retrieve every copy of the draft audit report and destroy them or instruct the individuals who had copies to do so. An Avon internal auditor was sent to China to gather additional information regarding Avon China executives' practice of bestowing gifts on Chinese government officials. The auditor was instructed by an Avon executive not to create any electronic records or send any emails when gathering this information, and not to mention the FCPA in any documents or emails. The internal auditor gathered the requested information, further documenting gifts to officials, and turned in two handwritten sheets of paper to an Avon executive, who then hand-carried the sheets to Avon's headquarters in New York.

Two executives, one from Avon and one from Avon China, discussed hiding an off-book record with names of recipients and details of the gifts at the Avon China executive's home. Ultimately, they decided against this. An Avon attorney provided Avon China the FCPA compliance language to add to future contracts with the consulting company, though the contracts were never updated to include the antibribery terms.

Neither Avon nor Avon China executives put in place controls to prevent the conduct or to ensure the accuracy of Avon China's books and records. A year later, Avon's internal auditors again reviewed the travel and entertainment and discretionary expenses for Avon China and found that the practices had continued. Still Avon took no steps to prevent Avon China from giving gifts to government officials. In 2007, an Avon executive reported to the company's compliance committee that inquiry into the potential FCPA violations by Avon China had been closed as "unsubstantiated," even though the executive and others knew that Avon China's practice of giving gifts to government officials and falsely recording them in the books was ongoing. Yet for each of the years that this behavior persisted, until September 2008, Avon China executives signed letters to their external auditor stating that Avon China's books and records were fair and accurate.

THE RESOLUTION

In 2008, the company reported itself to the Securities and Exchange Commission (SEC). But it wasn't until 2014 that the Justice Department and the SEC completed their investigations and negotiations with Avon to resolve the dual-enforcement actions.

On the criminal side, Avon China pleaded guilty to conspiracy to violate the FCPA by hiding more than $8 million in gifts to Chinese officials. Under the terms of a deferred prosecution agreement, Avon, the parent company, was charged in a criminal information with conspiring to violate the books-and-records provisions and with violating the internal controls provisions of the FCPA. That criminal case was held in abeyance under the terms of the deferred prosecution agreements, and the government agreed to dismiss the two criminal charges if Avon complied with the terms of the settlement. As part of the settlement, Avon agreed to pay a total of $135 million in fines and penalties and to revamp its compliance regulations and procedures, a process to be overseen by an independent monitor for eighteen months. Part of that $135 million included, under the terms of an SEC civil settlement, Avon's disgorgement of $67 million in benefits that resulted from the misconduct (SEC, 2014). Parent company Avon disclosed that it had also spent more than $300 million in professional fees to investigate itself, including any improper payments made in countries beyond China, in an effort to show a high level of cooperation with the government (Henning, 2014).

Avon's settlement was the third largest FCPA enforcement action resolved in 2014, according to the "FCPA Digest," an annual report compiled by the law firm Shearman & Sterling, LLP. The two largest settlements that year included a $384 million settlement by Alcoa Inc. and a subsidiary for a bribery scheme in the kingdom of Bahrain, and a $772 million settlement by Alstom S.A., a French power and transportation company, for a widespread bribery scheme involving tens of millions of dollars in bribes in Indonesia, Saudi Arabia, Egypt, and the Bahamas. Although the financial penalty for Avon was a fraction of those in the larger cases, Avon was the only defendant in 2014 required to retain an independent monitor (Sherman & Sterling, 2019). That imposition may reflect the "striking compliance failures, including an effort by company executives to cover up (or at a minimum, turn a blind eye to) Avon China's practice of offering government officials improper benefits and the allegations suggesting that the legal and compliance department failed in its role to ensure improper conduct was investigated and stopped" (Sherman & Sterling, 2019, p. 5).

The SEC and Justice Department have many tools available for resolving FCPA cases, including plea agreements, deferred prosecution agreements, and nonprosecution agreements. The agencies can also settle charges without requiring those agreements, which hold over the company at least a threat of criminal charges. A guilty plea is the harshest penalty, as it carries the most severe collateral consequences, including harm to a company's reputation or brand, disqualification from government procurement processes, and potential risks in private civil litigation (Sherman & Sterling, 2019). The government is "sensitive to these issues and helps corporations avoid the worst of these [consequences] by structuring the pleas with subsidiaries rather than the parent entities" (Sherman & Sterling, 2019, p. 4). This was the case in the Avon settlement, where Avon China entered the guilty plea, and the parent company signed a deferred prosecution agreement, under the terms of which the criminal charge was dismissed at the end of the supervision period.

Deferred or nonprosecution agreements, wherein the company admits to the facts and agrees to pay the penalties, generally also require the company to cooperate with the government's investigation. That can include investigation into individual employees' criminal liability for FCPA violations. Under a 2015 policy, the Department of Justice took the position that for corporations seeking credit for cooperation in a criminal investigation must provide

United States Sentencing Guidelines (2018)

The United States Sentencing Guidelines (USSG) provide a starting point for determining the sentence in any federal criminal conviction. But for corporate defendants, the Guidelines have special rules that take into account several factors. In determining a sentence, the court looks at whether the organization was primarily for a criminal purpose; if so, the Guidelines direct that the fine should be sufficiently high to deplete the organization's assets (USSG, Introductory Commentary). The court must also determine the seriousness of the criminal conduct, the culpability of the corporate entity, and whether it is appropriate to impose a sentence of probation to reduce the likelihood of future criminal conduct.

The first priority, though, is to order the corporate defendant to remedy harm caused by the criminal offense (USSG, Introductory Commentary). This is a priority because it affords a way for the victims to be made whole—and it's not considered punishment, but only restitution to those harmed.

Below is an excerpt of section 8 of the United States Sentencing Guidelines, addressing sentencing of organizations. The parts that follow address restitution and remedial orders.

Part B. Remedy Harm from Criminal Conduct, and Effective Compliance and Ethics Program

1. Remedying Harm from Criminal Conduct

Introductory Commentary

As a general principle, the court should require that the organization take all appropriate steps to provide compensation to victims and otherwise remedy the harm caused or threatened by the offense. A restitution order or an order of probation requiring restitution can be used to compensate identifiable victims of the offense. A remedial order or an order of probation requiring community service can be used to reduce or eliminate the harm threatened, or to repair the harm caused by the offense, when that harm or threatened harm would otherwise not be remedied. An order of notice to victims can be used to notify unidentified victims of the offense.

§8B1.1. Restitution—Organizations

(a) In the case of an identifiable victim, the court shall—

(1) enter a restitution order for the full amount of the victim's loss, if such order is authorized . . . ; or

(2) impose a term of probation or supervised release with a condition requiring restitution for the full amount of the victim's loss, if the offense is not an offense for which restitution is authorized under 18 U.S.C. § 3663(a)(1) but otherwise meets the criteria for an order of restitution under that section.

(b) *Provided,* that the provisions of subsection (a) do not apply—

(1) when full restitution has been made; or

(2) in the case of a restitution order under § 3663; a restitution order under 18 U.S.C. § 3663A that pertains to an offense against property . . . or a condition of restitution imposed pursuant to subsection (a)(2) above, to the extent the court finds, from facts on the record, that (A) the number of identifiable victims is so large as to make restitution impracticable; or (B) determining complex issues of fact related to the cause or amount of the victim's losses would complicate or prolong the sentencing process to a degree that the need to provide restitution to any victim is outweighed by the burden on the sentencing process.

(c) If a defendant is ordered to make restitution to an identifiable victim and to pay a fine, the court shall order that any money paid by the defendant shall first be applied to satisfy the order of restitution.

(d) A restitution order may direct the defendant to make a single, lump sum payment, partial payments at specified intervals, in-kind payments, or a combination of payments at specified intervals and in-kind payments. . . . An in-kind payment may be in the form of (1) return of property; (2) replacement of property; or (3) if the victim agrees, services rendered to the victim or to a person or organization other than the victim. . . .

(e) A restitution order may direct the defendant to make nominal periodic payments if the court finds from facts on the record that the economic circumstances of the defendant do not allow the payment of any amount of a restitution order, and do not allow for the payment of the full amount of a restitution order in the foreseeable future under any reasonable schedule of payments.

§ 8B1.2. Remedial Orders—Organizations (Policy Statement)

(a) To the extent not addressed under § 8B1.1 (Restitution—Organizations), a remedial order imposed as a condition of probation may require the organization to remedy the harm caused by the offense and to eliminate or reduce the risk that the instant offense will cause future harm.

(b) If the magnitude of expected future harm can be reasonably estimated, the court may require the organization to create a trust fund sufficient to address that expected harm.

Commentary

Background: The purposes of a remedial order are to remedy harm that has already occurred and to prevent future harm. A remedial order requiring corrective action by the organization may be necessary to prevent future injury from the instant offense, e.g. a product recall for a food and drug violation or a clean-up order for an environmental violation. In some cases in which a remedial order potentially may be appropriate, a governmental regulatory agency, e.g. the Environmental Protection Agency or the Food and Drug Administration, may have authority to order remedial measures. In such cases, a remedial order by the court may not be necessary. If a remedial order is entered, it should be coordinated with any administrative or civil actions taken by the appropriate governmental regulatory agency.

the DOJ with "all relevant facts about the individuals involved in corporate misconduct" (Yates, 2015, p. 3). The department would focus on individuals at all stages of the investigation into a corporation's criminal wrongdoing, and, absent extraordinary circumstances, corporate settlements would not shield executives or other employees from prosecution. Holding individuals accountable for criminal conduct in a corporate setting, the DOJ asserted, "is important for several reasons: it deters future illegal activity, it incentivizes changes in corporate behavior, it ensures that the proper parties are held responsible for their actions, and it promotes the public's confidence in our justice system" (Yates, 2015, p. 1). This policy was softened in 2018 under a new administration, as seen in the speech excerpted in this chapter by then deputy attorney general Rod Rosenstein.

In the Avon case, no individuals were charged with criminal wrongdoing.

REFERENCES

Albanese, J. (2011). *Transnational Crime and the 21st Century: Criminal Enterprise, Corruption, and Opportunity.* New York: Oxford University Press.

Deferred Prosecution Agreement. (2014). United States v. Avon Products, Inc. S. Dist. New York. December 15.

DOJ OPA (Department of Justice, Office of Public Affairs). (September 27, 2018). "Petróleo Brasileiro S.A.—Petrobras Agrees to Pay More Than $850 Million for FCPA Violations." United States Department of Justice. https://www.justice .gov/opa/pr/petr-leo-brasileiro-sa-petrobras-agrees-pay-more-850-million-fcpa-violations.

DOJ OPA (Department of Justice, Office of Public Affairs). (June 4, 2018). "Société Générale S.A. Agrees to Pay $860 Million in Criminal Penalties for Bribing Gaddafi-Era Libyan Officials and Manipulating LIBOR Rate." United States Department of Justice. https://www.justice.gov/opa/pr/soci-t-g-n-rale-sa-agrees-pay-860-million-criminal-penalties-bribing-gaddafi-era-libyan.

Henning, P. (2014). "Foreign Bribery Cases That Can Drag On and On." *New York Times,* December 22. https://nyti.ms/2lD5Jfw.

O'Sullivan, J. (2012). *Federal White Collar Crime.* 5th edition. St. Paul, MN: West.

Rosenstein, R. (2017). "Deputy Attorney General Rosenstein Delivers Remarks at the 34th International Conference on the Foreign Corrupt Practices Act." United States Department of Justice. November 29. https://www.justice.gov /opa/speech/deputy-attorney-general-rosenstein-delivers-remarks-34th-international-conference-foreign.

SEC. (2014). "SEC Charges Avon with FCPA Violations." U.S. Securities and Exchange Commission. December 17. https://www.sec.gov/news/pressrelease /2014-285.html.

SEC. (2018). "Panasonic Charged with FCPA and Accounting Fraud Violations." U.S. Securities and Exchange Commission. April 30. https://www.sec.gov/news /press-release/2018-73.

Sherman & Sterling. (2019). "FCPA Digest: Cases and Review Release Relating to Bribes to Foreign Officials under the Foreign Corrupt Practices Act of 1977.

Shearman. January. https://www.shearman.com/perspectives/2019/01/shearman-fcpa-digest-2019-and-recent-trends-and-patterns-in-fcpa.

Yates, Sally Quillian. (2015). Memorandum for the Assistant Attorney General, Antitrust Division [et al.], Subject: Individual Accountability for Corporate Wrongdoing. United States Department of Justice. September 9. https://www.justice.gov/archives/dag/file/769036/download.

TEN

Insider Trading

UNITED STATES V. DONALD J.

IN LATE DECEMBER 2001, ImClone founder and CEO Sam Waksal received some bad news: the US Food and Drug Administration had declined the pharmaceutical company's application to approve its drug Erbitux for treatment in late-stage colorectal cancer (White and Gillis, 2002). It was the type of news that could send a company's stock price into a nosedive. Waksal told his daughter to sell her 40,000 ImClone shares. The news was made public a few days later and, predictably, ImClone's stock price dropped. Waksal pleaded guilty in October 2002 to six federal charges, including securities fraud, obstruction of justice, perjury, and bank fraud, and was sentenced in June 2003 to 7 years in prison.

Sam Waksal's case illustrates a common insider-trading scenario: an insider gains material, confidential information and tips off a third party who acts on that news before it's made public and can affect the stock price. The Waksal case is known less for its educational value, though, than for spawning a white-collar criminal case against a Waksal friend, Martha Stewart, CEO of Martha Stewart Living, the media company and promoter of a popular line of home goods. Stewart's case grabbed media attention for insider trading, though she was not charged with selling her shares of ImClone prior to the FDA news based on inside information from Waksal. Rather, she was charged with, and later convicted of, lying to investigators about the reason for her sale of ImClone stock (Scannell and Rose, 2004). Stewart eventually served 5 months in prison, followed by 5 months of home confinement. Despite not being charged or convicted of insider trading, Martha Stewart is the first name that comes to mind for many people when talking about this crime.

To convict a defendant of insider trading, the government must prove that the defendant shared or stole material, nonpublic information and traded on that information to personally profit. The confidential information may be about pending takeovers or mergers, changes in key executives, mixed or weak quarterly reports, or as-yet-unrevealed details on new products, such as a pending FDA approval for a new drug. Often these cases involve multiple parties, as one person who has the information passes on a tip to someone else, usually unrelated to the tipper's company, and that person conducts a trade. The case in this chapter illustrates another scenario, one in which an individual doesn't tip off anyone else but acts on the information by himself.

One of the more difficult problems that insider trading involves is determining who is the victim. That was an issue debated in the following case, where a NASDAQ manager was accused of trading on information accessed through his job. As you read the following case, think about who is harmed when insider trading occurs. Is insider trading a victimless crime, or is it a crime against society? And, if so, what is the best way to determine a sentence when federal guidelines for sentencing rely so heavily on the loss?

"A FOX IN A HEN-HOUSE"

By all accounts, Donald J. was a pleasure to work with over his nearly twenty-year career at the NASDAQ Stock Market (Strasburg, Lucchetti, and Eaglesham, 2011). He came to Wall Street in 1989, after spending six years as a nurse in the United States Army, and by 2006 had worked his way up to a position as a managing director of the NASDAQ's market intelligence desk. Donald and his colleagues on the market intelligence desk analyzed trading to understand how different forces affected stocks and sectors of the market, and offered NASDAQ-listed companies data and analysis about how their shares traded. As a part of the job, Donald regularly received confidential information, such as departures of key executives, earnings reports, and advance notice of approvals of pharmaceutical products, or other market-making news. Those types of information are critical to investors and can drive a company's share price higher or lower—sometimes significantly.

To prevent such sensitive information from being misused, all NASDAQ employees are required to disclose their personal trading accounts, as well as those of their family members. But in 2006, Donald began making trades in an undisclosed investment account under his wife's name. At the time, Donald's salary was approximately $141,000 per year, but the *Wall Street Journal* reported that, considering annual bonuses, his income was about

$300,000 a year (Strasburg, Lucchetti, and Eaglesham, 2011). He and his wife owned two homes—one in Virginia and the other in Puerto Rico.

Because his job involved helping companies analyze how news would affect the trading of their stock, he was often privy to private and material information. But Donald also urged company representatives to share information with him (Complaint, 2011). When the confidential information was positive and would likely result in the stock price rising, Donald would purchase shares in the company shortly before the announcement. Once the news was made public, he would sell the shares he'd purchased at a profit (Government's Position on Sentencing, 2011).

For example, Donald learned that United Therapeutics Corp. (UTHR), a pharmaceutical company, would be announcing a successful trial result for a drug and, using that information, he invested in UTHR shares. Soon after the announcement, he sold the shares and generated $175,000 in profit. Two years later, Donald learned of another positive development for UTHR—the company received an email notification that the FDA had approved its drug Tyvaso for treatment of pulmonary arterial hypertension. UTHR's general counsel forwarded the email and letter to Donald, who was advising the company on how to best release the information publicly if the news came during the trading day, when markets were open (Complaint, 2011). Four minutes after receiving the approval letter by email, Donald purchased 11,500 shares of UTHR stock using his wife's account on his work computer. Ninety minutes after the FDA email arrived, UTHR made the information public in a press release. The company's stock surged by nearly $10, and closed 12 percent higher than the prior day's closing. Donald sold his shares an hour after he bought them and made a profit of approximately $110,000.

If the company's pending announcement was expected to have a negative effect on the stock price, Donald would bet against the stock by selling shares short. In short-selling, an investor borrows shares of the stock and then immediately sells the shares, essentially betting that the price of the stock will go down. If the price of the stock price falls, the investor buys the shares at a lower price to return them to the lender and pocket the difference.

In one short-sale transaction, Donald profited by $34,047 by shorting stock in Digene Corp. prior to its announcement that a key executive—the company's cofounder, chief operating officer, and chief financial officer—was resigning. In October 2008, Donald asked a representative from Idexx Laboratories Inc. to share pending earning results with him so he could better advise the company about how the market would react to the news.

Donald assured the representative that "he could not use information in any improper way" (Complaint, 2011, p. 9). After learning that the earnings report would be mixed—they would be in line with expectations, but future earnings would likely not rise as much as expected—Donald then used that information to short-sell 15,500 shares of Idexx. The next day, after the earnings report was released, Donald covered the short position, profiting by approximately $99,000. In another, similar transaction, Donald learned that a company was about to announce a mixed report of earnings in line with estimates, though revenues were weaker than expected. Donald used the information to short-sell the stock before the announcement, covered his short position, and generated more than $100,000 in gains.

Donald's trades were relatively small and infrequent. But they were also bold. He made several trades from his NASDAQ work computer, working side by side with his colleagues. In all, Donald earned profits of about $755,000 on fewer than a dozen trades from 2006 until he retired in 2009.

Before his retirement, however, Donald suffered trading losses that largely wiped out the gains he had made using the inside information. Later, the Financial Industry Regulatory Authority (FINRA), the private corporation that oversees US broker-dealers, detected suspicious activities in Donald's wife's account and referred the matter to the Securities and Exchange Commission (SEC).

CIVIL AND CRIMINAL PROSECUTIONS

In December 2010, inspectors from the US Postal Inspection Service arrived at Donald's home and presented him with the preliminary findings of the Department of Justice and the SEC (Defendant's Position on Sentencing, 2011). He immediately admitted what he had done (Government's Position on Sentencing, 2011). In May 2011, Donald pleaded guilty to one count of securities fraud, a violation of 15 U.S.C. §§ 78j(b) and 78ff (Information, 2011).

The defendant "was a fox in a hen-house," as Assistant US Attorney Lanny Breuer put it in a press release. "NASDAQ-listed companies entrusted him with their sensitive, non-public information so that he could provide them with analyses about their stock. He then used that very information to cheat the system and make an illegal profit. Insider trading by a gatekeeper on a securities exchange is a shocking abuse of trust, and must be punished. The integrity of our securities markets is vital to the U.S. economy, and the Justice Department is determined to take on insider trading at every level" (DOJ OPA, 2011).

The insider-trading charge carries a sentencing range between zero and 20 years of imprisonment and a fine of up to $5 million, or both. Under the terms of his plea agreement, the prosecutors and the defendant agreed to certain provisions of the United States Sentencing Guidelines, which is the starting point for determining a sentence (Plea Agreement, 2011). In cases involving financial crimes, the sentence is largely driven by the loss amount. Because it is difficult to calculate a loss in insider trading cases, the Guidelines direct that the illicit gain should be considered instead (USSG § 2B1.4, Commentary).

The parties agreed that the gain was between $400,000 and $1 million and that because Donald had pleaded guilty, he should receive consideration for acceptance of responsibility, which would lower the advisory sentencing range. Donald also agreed to forfeit the profits he earned. The parties did not agree about whether Donald's sentence should be increased for abusing a position of special trust.

At the sentencing hearing in August 2011, Donald's attorney argued for 18 months in prison, followed by 12 months of home confinement (Defendant's Position on Sentencing, 2011). In arguing for a lenient sentence, Donald's attorney stressed that his client had not abused a position of trust and, therefore, his sentence should not be increased because of that aggravating factor. In insider-trading cases, it can be difficult if not impossible to identify a victim who suffered direct harm. To increase his sentence, the government needed to prove that Donald had a position of special trust with an individual and then abused that relationship.

Donald's attorneys argued that insider trading is a crime without victims. There was no evidence that the market was affected by the news of Donald's arrest, and his attorneys pointed to studies that showed insider-trading cases did not decrease market liquidity or lower investor confidence (Defendant's Position on Sentencing, 2011). If there were any victims of insider trading, it might be the parties with whom Donald had traded, as those persons would have been at a disadvantage. However, Donald's attorneys argued, there was no evidence to indicate that those parties had been harmed. Even if they could show harm, Donald had not been in a trust relationship with those individuals, nor did he owe them a fiduciary duty.

Given his personal history and characteristics, his lawyers argued, Donald did not require a lengthy prison sentence to be deterred from future crimes.

SENTENCING GUIDELINES

The United States Sentencing Guidelines (USSG) are used to calculate an advisory sentencing range. The Guidelines assign a base level to an offense, then add levels for aggravating factors, such as the number of victims or the loss amount in a fraud case. Where there are mitigating factors, a certain number of levels are subtracted. For example, a defendant who pleads guilty instead of going to trial may receive a two- or three-level reduction.

The Guidelines also account for a defendant's prior criminal history in determining which Criminal History category they fall into. When both of these calculations are complete, an advisory sentencing range is determined on the Sentencing Table, a grid that sets out ranges in months. Offense levels are along the vertical axis, and criminal history categories (I–VI) form the horizontal axis. (See USSG, Sentencing Table).

The federal sentencing statute, 18 U.S.C. § 3553(a), directs a sentencing judge to impose a sentence that is "sufficient, but not greater than necessary" to achieve the goals of sentencing as set forth in the statute. Determining the correct advisory sentencing range under the Guidelines is the first step in determining a sentence.

§ 2B1.4. Insider Trading

(a) Base Offense Level: 8

(b) Specific Offense Characteristics

(1) If the gain resulting from the offense exceeded $6,500, increase by the number of levels from the table in § 2B1.1 (Theft, Property Destruction, and Fraud) corresponding to that amount.

(2) If the offense involved an organized scheme to engage in insider trading and the offense level determined above is less than level **14**, increase to level **14**.

Commentary

Application Notes:

1. *Application of Subsection (b)(2).* For purposes of subsection (b)(2), an "organized scheme to engage in insider trading" means a scheme to engage in insider trading that involves considered, calculated, sys-

tematic, or repeated efforts to obtain and trade on inside information, as distinguished from fortuitous or opportunistic instances of insider trading.

The following is a non-exhaustive list of factors that the court may consider in determining whether the offense involved an organized scheme to engage in insider trading:

(A) the number of transactions;

(B) the dollar value of the transactions;

(C) the number of securities involved;

(D) the duration of the offense;

(E) the number of participants in the scheme (although such a scheme may exist even in the absence of more than one participant);

(F) the efforts undertaken to obtain material, nonpublic information;

(G) the number of instances in which material, nonpublic information was obtained; and

(H) the efforts undertaken to conceal the offense.

2. *Application of § 3B1.3.* Section 3B1.3 (Abuse of Position of Trust or Use of Special Skill) should be applied if the defendant occupied and abused a position of special trust. Examples might include a corporate president or an attorney who misused information regarding a planned but unannounced takeover attempt. It typically would not apply to an ordinary "tippee."

Furthermore, § 3B1.3 should be applied if the defendant's employment in a position that involved regular participation or professional assistance in creating, issuing, buying, selling, or trading securities or commodities was used to facilitate significantly the commission or concealment of the offense. It would apply, for example, to a hedge fund professional who regularly participates in securities transactions or to a lawyer who regularly provides professional assistance in securities transactions, if the defendant's employment in such a position was used to facilitate significantly the commission or concealment of the offense. It ordinarily would not apply to a position such as a clerical worker in an investment firm, because such a position ordinarily does not involve special skill. *See* § 3B1.3, comment. (n. 4).

Background: This guideline applies to certain violations of Rule 10b-5 that are commonly referred to as "insider trading." Insider trading

> is treated essentially as a sophisticated fraud. Because the victims and their losses are difficult if not impossible to identify, the gain, *i.e.,* the total increase in value realized through trading in securities by the defendant and persons acting in concert with the defendant or to whom the defendant provided inside information, is employed instead of the victims' losses.

At the time of sentencing, he was fifty-seven years old, married, and had three adult children. His profits from the insider-trading scheme were nullified by his losses on the stock market, and he was facing a certain prison sentence as well as a civil lawsuit by the SEC that also named his wife as a relief defendant. He cited a lengthy history of charitable work, including volunteering to provide medical assistance in Haiti following the earthquake and cholera epidemic in 2010. And he was facing "crushing" penalties and disgorgement. In a letter to the court, Donald noted that he "never desired or lived a lavish lifestyle—nor is there any evidence that anyone in my family had a rapacious desire for wealth or material items" (Defendant's Position on Sentencing, 2011, p. 2). As an individual who had never faced legal trouble before, a sentence of 18 months, followed by a year of home confinement, was sufficient, his attorneys argued, to deter Donald and others from committing similar crimes, and was in line with other insider-trading sentences (Defendant's Position on Sentencing, 2011).

The government agreed that Donald had taken responsibility for his actions immediately upon being confronted with the evidence against him, but prosecutors argued that as a manager on the market intelligence desk, Donald did have a fiduciary duty to not trade on inside information. As the prosecutors noted in their sentencing brief, the United States Sentencing Guidelines (USSG) address the intersection of insider trading and the abuse-of-trust enhancement. The enhancement for abuse of trust should be applied "only if the defendant occupied and abused a position of special trust" (USSG § 2B1.4, Note 2). And Donald's position as a manager was similar to the examples given: "a corporate president or an attorney who misused information regarding a planned but unannounced takeover attempt" (ibid.). The companies who worked with the NASDAQ intelligence desk "reported their most sensitive, insider information to the defendant precisely because of the special position he held" (Government's Position on Sentencing, 2011). The information provided to the defendant would normally be held closely and be shared only with the most senior corporate insiders, the government argued. By trading on the information for his own profit, the defendant abused that special trust.

Given their differing interpretations of how that trust enhancement should apply, the parties argued that different advisory sentencing ranges applied. The government argued that the advisory sentencing range under the Guidelines was 37 to 46 months. Donald's attorney calculated an advisory Guideline range of 30 to 37 months. The judge sentenced Donald to a term in the middle, 42 months in prison, and ordered that he forfeit $755,000.

The SEC's civil lawsuit against Donald and his wife sought disgorgement of illicit profits, along with interest and penalties, in addition to the forfeiture ordered in the criminal case. Donald's wife was dismissed from the civil suit in 2011. In 2014, Donald agreed to a judgment that found him liable for his illicit profits and imposed disgorgement in the amount of $755,000, plus $143,000 in interest. He was ordered to pay a total of $898,108 to the Securities and Exchange Commission (Final Judgment, 2014).

POSTSCRIPT

The Securities and Exchange Commission uses a variety of tools to detect insider trading, which can be a difficult crime to investigate and prove (Office of the Whistleblower). These efforts are important to preserving the public's trust in the market and ensuring that the financial markets are a level playing field for all who participate. The SEC uses market surveillance tools to look for unusual trading activity, particularly around the time of key corporate developments, such as the release of earnings reports. An extraordinarily significant transaction, such as buying or selling a large number of shares, may alert regulators and spark an investigation. Regulators also rely on tips and complaints. The SEC's Office of the Whistleblower welcomes tips about securities fraud, and if a tipster's information leads to an enforcement action that garners more than $1 million in sanctions, the whistleblower may be eligible for an award of between 10 percent and 30 percent of the money collected.

15 U.S.C. § 78j(b). Manipulative and Deceptive Devices

It shall be unlawful for any person, directly or indirectly, by the use of any means or instrumentality of interstate commerce or of the mails, or of any facility of any national securities exchange—
(a)

(1) To affect a short sale, or to use or employ any stop-loss order in connection with the purchase or sale, of any security other than a government security, in contravention of such rules and regulations as the Commission may prescribe as necessary or appropriate in the public interest or for the protection of investors.

(2) Paragraph (1) of this subsection shall not apply to security futures products.

(b) To use or employ, in connection with the purchase or sale of any security registered on a national securities exchange or any security not so registered, or any securities-based swap agreement any manipulative or deceptive device or contrivance in contravention of such rules and regulations as the Commission may prescribe as necessary or appropriate in the public interest or for the protection of investors.
(c)

(1) To affect, accept, or facilitate a transaction involving the loan or borrowing of securities in contravention of such rules and regulations as the Commission may prescribe as necessary or appropriate in the public interest or for the protection of investors.

(2) Nothing in paragraph (1) may be construed to limit the authority of the appropriate Federal banking agency (as defined in section 1813(q) of title 12), the National Credit Union Administration, or any other Federal department or agency having a responsibility under Federal law to prescribe rules or regulations restricting transactions involving the loan or borrowing of securities in order to protect the safety and soundness of a financial institution or to protect the financial system from systemic risk.

Rules promulgated under subsection (b) that prohibit fraud, manipulation, or insider trading (but not rules imposing or specifying reporting or recordkeeping requirements, procedures, or standards as prophylactic measures against fraud, manipulation, or insider trading), and judicial precedents decided under subsection (b) and rules promulgated thereunder that prohibit fraud, manipulation, or insider trading, shall apply to security-based swap agreements to the same extent as they apply to securities. Judicial precedents decided under section 77q(a) of this title and sections 78i, 78o, 78p, 78t, and 78u-1 of this title, and judicial precedents decided under applicable rules promulgated under such sections, shall apply to security-based swap agreements to the same extent as they apply to securities.

15 U.S.C. § 78ff. Penalties

(a) Willful violations; false and misleading statements

Any person who willfully violates any provision of this chapter . . ., or any rule or regulation thereunder the violation of which is made unlawful or the observance of which is required under the terms of this chapter, or any person who willfully and knowingly makes, or causes to be made, any statement in any application, report, or document required to be filed under this chapter or any rule or regulation thereunder or any undertaking contained in a registration statement as provided in subsection (d) of section 78o of this title, or by any self-regulatory organization in connection with an application for membership or participation therein or to become associated with a member thereof, which statement was false or misleading with respect to any material fact, shall upon conviction be fined not more than $5,000,000, or imprisoned not more than 20 years, or both, except that when such person is a person other than a natural person, a fine not exceeding $25,000,000 may be imposed; but no person shall be subject to imprisonment under this section for the violation of any rule or regulation if he proves that he had no knowledge of such rule or regulation.

(b) Failure to file information, documents, or reports

Any issuer which fails to file information, documents, or reports required to be filed under subsection (d) of section 78o of this title or any rule or regulation thereunder shall forfeit to the United States the sum of $100 for each and every day such failure to file shall continue. Such forfeiture, which shall be in lieu of any criminal penalty for such failure to file which might

be deemed to arise under subsection (a) of this section, shall
be payable into the Treasury of the United States and shall be
recoverable in a civil suit in the name of the United States.
(c) Violations by issuers, officers, directors, stockholders, employees,
or agents of issuers

(1)

(A) Any issuer that violates subsection (a) or (g) of section
78dd-1 of this title shall be fined not more than $2,000,000.

(B) Any issuer that violates subsection (a) or (g) of section
78dd-1 of this title shall be subject to a civil penalty of not more
than $10,000 imposed in an action brought by the Commission.

(2)

(A) Any officer, director, employee, or agent of an issuer, or
stockholder acting on behalf of such issuer, who willfully violates subsection (a) or (g) of section 78dd-1 of this title shall be
fined not more than $100,000, or imprisoned not more than 5
years, or both.

(B) Any officer, director, employee, or agent of an issuer, or
stockholder acting on behalf of such issuer, who violates subsection (a) or (g) of section 78dd-1 of this title shall be subject
to a civil penalty of not more than $10,000 imposed in an action
brought by the Commission.

(3) Whenever a fine is imposed under paragraph (2) upon any
officer, director, employee, agent, or stockholder of an issuer,
such fine may not be paid, directly or indirectly, by such issuer.

REFERENCES

Complaint. (2011). Securities and Exchange Commission v. Donald L. Johnson,
et al., 11-cv-03618. E. Dist. Virginia. May 26.

Defendant's Position on Sentencing. (2011) United States v. Donald Johnson, 11-cr-
00254. E. Dist. Virginia. August 7.

DOJ OPA (Department of Justice, Office of Public Affairs. (2011). "Former Nasdaq
Executive Pleads Guilty to Insider Trading." United States Department of Justice. May 26. https://www.justice.gov/opa/pr/former-nasdaq-executive-pleads-
guilty-insider-trading.

Final Judgment. (2014). Securities and Exchange Commission v. Donald L. Johnson, et al., 11-cv-03618. S. Dist. New York. November 12.

Government's Position on Sentencing. (2011). United States v. Donald Johnson, 11-cr-00254, E. Dist. Virginia. May 8.

Information. (2011). United States v. Donald Johnson, 11-cr-00254. E. Dist. Virginia. May 26.

Office of the Whistleblower. (n.d.). U.S. Securities and Exchange Commission. Accessed August 27, 2020. https://www.sec.gov/whistleblower.

Plea Agreement. (2011). United States v. Donald Johnson, 11-cr-00254. E. Dist. Virginia. May 26.

Scannell, K., and M. Rose. (2004). "Martha Stewart Is Found Guilty of All Charges." *Wall Street Journal*, March 7. https://www.wsj.com/articles /SB107833235519345426.

Strasburg, J., A. Lucchetti, and J. Eaglesham. (2011). "Inside Trader at Nasdaq Had Drug-Abuse Record." *Wall Street Journal,* June 10. https://www.wsj.com/articles /SB10001424052702304259304576373731829124842.

White, B., and J. Gillis (2002). "ImClone's Waksal Pleads Guilty to 6 Charges." *Washington Post*, October 16. https://www.washingtonpost.com/archive/politics /2002/10/16/imclones-waksal-pleads-guilty-to-6-charges/cd6af75b-19e7–4080-b971– 9bb33a4a824b/.

ELEVEN

Academic Fraud

UNITED STATES, ET AL. V. EDUCATION MANAGEMENT CORP., ET AL.

NO COMMUNITY IS EXEMPT FROM FRAUD OR ECONOMIC CRIMES, even the university community. Like industry and commerce, academia sees the usual financial misconduct—embezzlement, double-billing, false invoices, and the like. But colleges and universities can also experience some unique white-collar crimes, such as fraud related to academic research or collegiate sports. Professors, staff, administrators, and students can be victims of white-collar crimes on campus—or the perpetrators.

Few cases of academic fraud have caught the public attention like the 2019 arrests in a federal investigation called Operation Varsity Blues, which alleged a widespread effort to rig the college admissions process for children of wealthy and famous parents. More than fifty people were charged for their involvement in two schemes—one to cheat on standardized admissions tests, the other involving bribery of college officials to get students falsely admitted as athletes. The mastermind behind both schemes was William "Rick" Singer, who pleaded guilty and cooperated with the FBI in the investigation by recording his calls with dozens of parents who were trying to get their children into elite universities. The FBI investigation resulted in the arrests of dozens of parents, including actresses Felicity Huffman and Lori Loughlin and Loughlin's husband, fashion designer Mossimo Giannulli. Huffman pleaded guilty to paying $15,000 to Singer's nonprofit organization, The Key Worldwide Foundation, to have her daughter's SAT scores falsely inflated. Huffman was sentenced in September 2019 to 14 days in prison, 250 hours of community service, and a fine of $30,000. After negotiating an agreement to plead guilty, Loughlin was sentenced in August 2020 to a two-month prison sentence and Giannulli was sentenced to a five-month term (Taylor, 2020).

Other for-profit education companies sued for conduct similar to that involved in this chapter's case study include the following:

- DeVry University agreed to pay $100 million to settle a lawsuit brought by the Federal Trade Commission that alleged the school and its parent company misled students with advertisements that touted high employment and income levels after graduation (FTC, 2016). Under the settlement, DeVry paid $49.4 million to students who were harmed by the deceptive ads and provided $50.6 million in student debt relief.

- Trump University settled a class-action lawsuit brought by 3,730 former students who alleged that they were misled by recruiters who used high-pressure sales techniques and false claims about what they'd learn in the business courses. The company, owned by Donald Trump, did not admit wrongdoing, but agreed to pay $25 million to reimburse students for most of their tuition payments (Eder and Medina, 2017).

- University of Phoenix settled False Claims Act violations with a $67.5 million payment in a 2009 case that began as a whistle-blower action brought by two employees (DOJ OPA, 2009). The federal government did not intervene, but the two employees prevailed in settling this case about incentive-based compensation paid to recruiters. The two whistleblower employees received $19 million from the settlement.

- Education Affiliates (EA), which operated fifty campuses in the United States, agreed to pay $13 million in 2015 to settle allegations of False Claims Act violations (DOJ OPA, 2015). The US Department of Justice alleged that EA employees altered admissions test results, created false high school diplomas, and falsified students' federal aid applications in order to admit unqualified students who then were awarded federal financial aid that was paid to the schools. Two EA admission representatives and one test proctor were criminally convicted.

The case has resulted in several university athletics employees being put on administrative leave or terminated.

Most cases of white-collar crime on campus get far less attention. Professional misconduct, such as fraud related to research, may violate university regulations or academic standards, as in a case of plagiarism or falsifying data. In rare instances, that conduct rises to the level of criminal activity, such as the case of a medical researcher who admitted to faking results in an AIDS vaccine experiment (Leys, 2015). The apparent success of the researcher's experiment led to his university being awarded $20 million in federal grants. The scientist pleaded guilty to making false statements and was sentenced to 57 months in prison and restitution of $7.2 million.

But what happens when the university itself is the perpetrator of the fraud? That is the question at the core of this chapter's case study. It involves the False Claims Act (18 U.S.C. § 3279), a statute that allows private parties to initiate a civil lawsuit alleging the defendant has defrauded the federal government. The whistleblowers who uncover the fraud can receive up to 30 percent of the government's award if the lawsuit is successful.

As you read about the case of Education Management Corporation, a for-profit higher education company, think about who the victims were and how or whether this settlement addressed the harm inflicted by the conduct.

COLLEGE, INC.

In the mid- to late 2000s, Education Management Corporation (EDMC) was the second largest for-profit education company in the United States, receiving more than $11 billion in federal funds between 2003 and 2011 to educate students enrolled in its institutions (Joint Complaint, 2011). The company operated schools under four brands: Art Institutes, South University, Argosy University, and Brown-Mackie College. At the start of the April 2011 academic quarter, EDMC schools enrolled 148,800 students, many of whom participated in federally supported student loan and grant programs, such as federal Pell Grants, the Federal Family Education Loan Program (FFELP), and the Federal Direct Loan Program.

Pell Grants provide federal funds to students in financial need. To qualify, the students submit a Free Application for Federal Student Aid (FAFSA), and the Pell Grant amount is determined based on the expected contribution from the student's family. The student sends the FAFSA directly to the Department of Education, or the school transmits it to the DOE on the student's behalf. Using the information in the FAFSA, the school calculates the student's eligibility for aid and assembles a "financial aid award package" for the student borrower (Joint Complaint, 2011, p. 19). The financial aid package may include Pell Grants, federal direct loans, or campus-based aid, which may include Federal Supplemental Educational Opportunity grants, work-study, or federal Perkins loans, as well as other scholarships or aid for which the student may qualify (Joint Complaint, 2011, p. 20). The student can accept all or part of the financial aid package.

Under the FFELP, subsidized and unsubsidized Stafford loans are guaranteed by the government should a student default. The government pays the interest on a subsidized loan while the student is in school. Unsubsidized loans accrue interest while the student is still enrolled. Repayment on either type of loan does not start until several months after the student has either graduated or otherwise stopped attending the school.

For students to qualify for these federal loans or grants, the schools they enroll in must comply with specific conditions, including a restriction on how participating institutions recruit students. Universities and other vocational schools agree that they will not pay their employees a commission, bonus, or other incentive based on the number of students they enroll or for whom they secure financial aid. To maintain eligibility to receive federal funding, schools must provide the Department of Education with the institution's general-purpose financial statements. Each school must also certify that it is complying with all rules, including the regulation that bars recruitment- and retention-based commissions. These restrictions on paying bonuses came about after Congress noted that such payments correlated with high loan default rates, "which in turn resulted in a significant drain on program funds where the government acts as a loan guarantor" (Joint Complaint, 2011, p. 18).

EDMC RECRUITMENT PRACTICES

EDMC aggressively sought new students in its educational programs in ways that two former employees believed violated the Department of Education's regulations. In 2007, Lynntoya Washington, a recruiter for the Art Institute of Pittsburgh Online Division, filed a qui tam lawsuit alleging that EDMC had violated the False Claims Act (Joint Complaint, 2011). Washington had worked for EDMC for three years, primarily as associate director of admissions. A second former EDMC employee, Michael T. Mahoney, joined the case as a plaintiff in May 2011. Mahoney had been the director of training for EDMC's Online Higher Education Division for just under a year. In his position, Mahoney oversaw training of all online higher education admissions trainers, associate directors of admission, and admissions personnel.

A qui tam lawsuit may be brought under the False Claims Act and permits a private party to file suit alleging that the defendant has defrauded the federal government (31 U.S.C. § 3279 et seq.). These lawsuits are initially filed under seal, and the Department of Justice has a period in which to investigate and decide whether the government will intervene and take over the case. If the government decides to pursue the case and wins at trial or settles the lawsuit with the defendant, the whistleblower, who is known as a relator, receives between 15 and 25 percent of the award. If the government declines to pursue the case, the relator can continue the lawsuit and, if successful, may recover up to 30 percent of the government reward, though that amount may be less if the relator was involved in the fraud conduct. If the defendant is found liable for defrauding the government, the penalty can be up to treble damages (three times the amount of the fraud).

According to the complaint initiated by the two former employees, the company's associate directors of admission (ADAs) were trained to recruit applicants to EDMC schools and manage new-student inquiries and were given enrollment goals. Under the company's Admissions Performance Plan, compensation was based on an ADA's performance, which tracked the number and type of new students recruited in the prior year (Joint Complaint, 2011). To boost enrollment numbers, EDMC urged ADAs to admit students before thoroughly reviewing their transcripts to determine if they had the academic qualifications to attend the institution. The company also urged ADAs to enroll students who were unqualified, including those who could not write coherently, candidates who appeared to be under the influence of drugs, and applicants for online programs who did not own computers. Although the EDMC schools published academic requirements for incoming students, in practice the schools accepted any student who completed the application and submitted a 150-word essay. All student applications, regardless of the applicant's grade-point average or the quality of the written essay, were approved.

As part of the sales pitch, ADAs were instructed to tell prospective students that EDMC schools had "very high career placement percentages and that the Career Services Office will contact the student six weeks prior to graduation and will set up interviews for the student with prospective employers" and that graduates would have lifetime access to career assistance (Joint Complaint, 2011, p. 32). In reality, students had to initiate contact with the Career Services Office and could use those services for only a limited time after graduation.

One recruitment tactic that EDMC used was called "finding the pain," which meant looking for prospective students' vulnerabilities and then exploiting them to persuade the student to enroll (Joint Complaint, 2011, p. 33). Recruiters were trained to look for a potential student's goals, such as to increase income so a family could move to a safer neighborhood, or to make a father proud, and use those pressure points to convince the student to enroll, even if the person expressed a desire not to attend the school.

When students confirmed enrollment in their classes, they became financially liable to EDMC. That is also the point when an ADA would get credit for having recruited the student. In the week before the start of each quarter, ADAs received confirmation reports three times a day so they would know whether their students had confirmed their enrollment. If not, the ADA was expected to call and urge the student to confirm. Once students confirmed enrollment, whether they succeeded or failed in their classes no longer mattered to the ADA, because they had already earned their new-student credit for that enrollment.

The company used the same high-pressure sales tactics that ADAs used to recruit students to encourage the ADAs to meet their enrollment goals. Supervisors asked the ADAs to imagine their dream car or another financial goal or to name the overall salary they hoped to earn. The company used financial planning documents to show each ADA how many new student points were necessary to earn a certain salary (Joint Complaint, 2011, p. 37).

The top 10 percent of EDMC admissions personnel, based solely on the number of new students confirmed, were welcomed into the "President's Club" and were rewarded with all-expense-paid trips to Puerto Vallarta or Cancun, Mexico, or to Las Vegas. President's Club members could bring a family member or significant other on the trip at no cost. In addition, EDMC supervisors offered rewards on a short-term basis, giving top recruiters chocolates, movie and sports tickets, amusement park admissions, restaurant and Starbucks gift cards, and free lunches.

For-profit colleges play a vital role in higher education, expanding capacity beyond that of nonprofit and public college and university systems (HELP Committee, 2012). During times when states cut funding to public higher education, there was a corresponding growth in nontraditional students— those who attend part-time, who have delayed attending college, or who juggle families and full-time jobs. For-profit colleges often offer online options, convenient locations, and structured coursework that allows working students more flexibility. Hundreds of thousands of people have successfully completed degree programs with for-profit universities.

But a two-year investigation of for-profit colleges by the US Senate Committee on Health, Education, Labor, and Pensions (HELP Committee) found that these higher-education companies also charged higher tuition than their public counterparts, resulting in significant student loan debt for students who were mostly of modest means (HELP Committee, 2012). The committee's report found that 96 percent of students in for-profit schools took out student loans, compared to 13 percent of students enrolled in community colleges, 48 percent of those in four-year public schools, and 57 percent of those at four-year private nonprofit universities.

The for-profits schools also enrolled more high-dollar borrowers, with approximately 57 percent of students who earned a bachelor's degree graduating with $30,000 or more in debt. About 12 percent of graduates of four-year public institutions, and about 25 percent of those earning degrees at nonprofit private schools, carried that amount of debt.

For-profit schools had high dropout rates and high default rates on student loans. And as student loans are rarely discharged through bankruptcy, that debt can follow students for decades, creating a grave financial burden. Students who were unable to obtain financing through private lending companies, the HELP Committee found, could apply for loans through the educational institution, but those loans often carried high interest rates. The report noted that in 2009, seven for-profit college systems offered loans with interest rates between 11.2 percent and 18 percent. Stafford loans, which are guaranteed by the federal government, had an interest rate of 5.6 percent at that time.

The committee's investigation also uncovered aggressive, misleading, and sometimes deceptive recruiting practices: "Internal documentation, interviews with former employees, and Government Accountability Office (GAO) undercover recordings demonstrate that many companies used tactics that misled prospective students with regard to the cost of the program, the availability and obligations of Federal aid, the time to complete the program, the completion rates of other students, the job placement rates of other students, the transferability of the credit, or the reputation and accreditation of the school" (HELP Committee, 2012, p. 4).

Students who were enrolled in for-profit schools accounted for 47 percent of all defaults on federal student loans, and more than 20 percent of such students defaulted within three years of entering repayment on their loans. This figure is driven by students who drop out without completing a degree, then find themselves in debt and without the ability to repay.

The HELP Committee's report recommended that the Department of Education collect more and better information about student outcomes at for-profit schools, create a uniform method for calculating job placement rates, and increase the oversight of private lending and federal financial aid. It also recommended stronger protections for students, including the creation of an online student complaint clearinghouse and an extension of the ban on incentive compensation to all employees in higher education.

RESOLUTION WITH EDMC AND OTHER FOR-PROFIT COLLEGE COMPANIES

In 2011, the US Department of Justice and the attorneys general of California, Florida, Illinois, and Indiana intervened in the qui tam lawsuit, eventually reaching a settlement with EDMC in November 2015.

Under the settlement, EDMC did not admit any wrongdoing, but agreed to pay $95.5 million to resolve the charges that the higher-education company falsely claimed federal grant and loan funds in violation of the False Claims Act. In announcing the resolution of the case, US attorney general Loretta E. Lynch praised the bravery of the two employees who "blew the whistle on EDMC by alleging that it was running a high-pressure recruitment mill" (Lynch, 2015). Education Secretary Arne Duncan noted that 90 percent of the company's revenue came from federal education funding for EDMC students. He characterized the company's actions as lying to the federal government, but not lying to students (Lynch News Conference, 2015).

Critics of the settlement said it didn't go far enough in helping students or in recovering the $11 billion in student loan aid that the company received over the years. US senators Elizabeth Warren, Richard J. Durbin, and

Richard Blumenthal wrote that they were troubled that "no executive will go to jail, none will be sanctioned, and the settlement does not even contain an admission of wrongdoing by the company" (Warren, Durbin, Blumenthal, 2015, p. 2). Further, the senators were disappointed that the Department of Education had not automatically granted EDMC students debt relief, despite the department's ability to forgive student loans where an academic institution has engaged in fraudulent activities. The senators cited the DOJ complaint against the company, which had alleged that students took on unsustainable debt to enroll in educational programs for which they were not qualified or prepared to succeed in, all at the urging of EDMC's recruiters, which amounted to a violation of students' trust.

The same year as the EDMC settlement, the Department of Education expanded a program to forgive federal student loan debt to students who had attended Corinthian Colleges. Corinthian Colleges had been the largest for-profit education company in the nation before it abruptly closed its doors in April 2015 (Douglas-Gabriel, 2015). The closure followed a yearlong battle with the DOE over the company's recruitment practices and allegations of predatory lending. California attorney general Kamala Harris sued Corinthian Colleges in 2013, alleging that the for-profit education company, which operated Heald College, Everest College, and Wyotech, misrepresented job placement rates to students, ran ads for programs it didn't offer, and unlawfully used military seals in advertising (Complaint for Civil Penalties, 2013). In 2014, amidst allegations that the education company reported false graduation rates to the government, the Department of Education cut off the schools' access to federal funds, which made up about 85 percent of Corinthian's revenue.

The closure of about a hundred Corinthian campuses left nearly sixteen thousand students displaced. The collapse spurred the Department of Education in 2015 to update regulations governing loan forgiveness in cases where students have been defrauded by colleges, including a provision that would grant automatic debt cancelation to borrowers whose schools close. That policy was to take effect in June 2017 but was rejected by incoming education secretary Betsy DeVos before it could be implemented. A lawsuit by former students and state attorneys general resulted in the Trump administration agreeing to forgive $150 million in federal student aid tied to the college closures (Douglas-Gabriel, 2018).

The settlement that EDMC agreed to did not include forgiveness of federal student loans. However, the company reached agreements with state

STATUTE

31 U.S.C. § 3729. False Claims

(a) Liability for Certain Acts.—

(1) In general.—Subject to paragraph (2), any person who—

(A) knowingly presents, or causes to be presented, a false or fraudulent claim for payment or approval;

(B) knowingly makes, uses, or causes to be made or used, a false record or statement material to a false or fraudulent claim;

(C) conspires to commit a violation of subparagraph (A), (B), (D), (E), (F), or (G);

(D) has possession, custody, or control of property or money used, or to be used, by the Government and knowingly delivers, or causes to be delivered, less than all of that money or property;

(E) is authorized to make or deliver a document certifying receipt of property used, or to be used, by the Government and, intending to defraud the Government, makes or delivers the receipt without completely knowing that the information on the receipt is true;

(F) knowingly buys, or receives as a pledge of an obligation or debt, public property from an officer or employee of the Government, or a member of the Armed Forces, who lawfully may not sell or pledge property; or

(G) knowingly makes, uses, or causes to be made or used, a false record or statement material to an obligation to pay or transmit money or property to the Government, or knowingly conceals or knowingly and improperly avoids or decreases an obligation to pay or transmit money or property to the Government, is liable to the United States Government for a civil penalty of not less than $5,000 and not more than $10,000, as adjusted by the Federal Civil Penalties Inflation Adjustment Act of 1990 . . ., plus 3 times the amount of damages which the Government sustains because of the act of that person.

(2) Reduced damages.—If the court finds that—

(A) the person committing the violation of this subsection furnished officials of the United States responsible for investigating false claims violations with all information known to such person about the violation within 30 days after the date on which the defendant first obtained the information;

(B) such person fully cooperated with any Government investigation of such violation; and

(C) at the time such person furnished the United States with the information about the violation, no criminal prosecution, civil action, or administrative action had commenced under this title with respect to such violation, and the person did not have actual knowledge of the existence of an investigation into such violation,the court may assess not less than 2 times the amount of damages which the Government sustains because of the act of that person.

(3) Costs of civil actions.—

A person violating this subsection shall also be liable to the United States Government for the costs of a civil action brought to recover any such penalty or damages.

31 U.S.C. § 3730. Civil Actions for False Claims

(a) Responsibilities of the Attorney General.—

The Attorney General diligently shall investigate a violation under section 3729. If the Attorney General finds that a person has violated or is violating section 3729, the Attorney General may bring a civil action under this section against the person.

(b)Actions by Private Persons.—

(1) A person may bring a civil action for a violation of section 3729 for the person and for the United States Government. The action shall be brought in the name of the Government. The action may be dismissed only if the court and the Attorney General give written consent to the dismissal and their reasons for consenting.

(2) A copy of the complaint and written disclosure of substantially all material evidence and information the person possesses shall be served on the Government pursuant to Rule 4(d)(4) [1] of the Federal Rules of Civil Procedure. The complaint shall be filed in camera, shall remain under seal for at least 60 days, and shall not be served on the defendant until the court so orders. The Government may elect to intervene and proceed with the action within 60 days after it receives both the complaint and the material evidence and information.

(3) The Government may, for good cause shown, move the court for extensions of the time during which the complaint remains under seal under paragraph (2). Any such motions may be supported by affidavits or other submissions in camera. The defendant shall not be required to respond to any complaint filed under this section until 20 days after the complaint is unsealed and served upon the defendant pursuant to Rule 4 of the Federal Rules of Civil Procedure.

(4) Before the expiration of the 60-day period or any extensions obtained under paragraph (3), the Government shall—

(A) proceed with the action, in which case the action shall be conducted by the Government; or

(B) notify the court that it declines to take over the action, in which case the person bringing the action shall have the right to conduct the action.

(5) When a person brings an action under this subsection, no person other than the Government may intervene or bring a related action based on the facts underlying the pending action.

(c) Rights of the Parties to Qui Tam Actions.—

(1) If the Government proceeds with the action, it shall have the primary responsibility for prosecuting the action, and shall not be bound by an act of the person bringing the action. Such person shall have the right to continue as a party to the action, subject to the limitations set forth in paragraph (2).

(2)

(A) The Government may dismiss the action notwithstanding the objections of the person initiating the action if the person has been notified by the Government of the filing of the motion and the court has provided the person with an opportunity for a hearing on the motion.

(B) The Government may settle the action with the defendant notwithstanding the objections of the person initiating the action if the court determines, after a hearing, that the proposed settlement is fair, adequate, and reasonable under all the circumstances. Upon a showing of good cause, such hearing may be held in camera.

. . .

(3) If the Government elects not to proceed with the action, the person who initiated the action shall have the right to conduct the action. If the Government so requests, it shall be served with copies of all pleadings filed in the action and shall be supplied with copies of all deposition transcripts (at the Government's expense). When a person proceeds with the action, the court, without limiting the status and rights of the person initiating the action, may nevertheless permit the Government to intervene at a later date upon a showing of good cause.

(4) Whether or not the Government proceeds with the action, upon a showing by the Government that certain actions of discovery by the person initiating the action would interfere with the Government's investigation or prosecution of a criminal or civil matter arising out of the same facts, the court may stay such discovery for a period of not more than 60 days. Such a showing shall be conducted in camera. The court may extend the 60-day period upon a further showing in camera that the Government has pursued the criminal or civil investigation or proceedings with reasonable diligence and any proposed discovery in the civil action will interfere with the ongoing criminal or civil investigation or proceedings.

(5) Notwithstanding subsection (b), the Government may elect to pursue its claim through any alternate remedy available to the Government, including any administrative proceeding to determine a civil money penalty. If any such alternate remedy is pursued in another proceeding, the person initiating the action shall have the same rights in such proceeding as such person would have had if the action had continued under this section. Any finding of fact or conclusion of law made in such other pro-

ceeding that has become final shall be conclusive on all parties to an action under this section. For purposes of the preceding sentence, a finding or conclusion is final if it has been finally determined on appeal to the appropriate court of the United States, if all time for filing such an appeal with respect to the finding or conclusion has expired, or if the finding or conclusion is not subject to judicial review.

(d) Award to Qui Tam Plaintiff.—

(1) If the Government proceeds with an action brought by a person under subsection (b), such person shall, subject to the second sentence of this paragraph, receive at least 15 percent but not more than 25 percent of the proceeds of the action or settlement of the claim, depending upon the extent to which the person substantially contributed to the prosecution of the action. Where the action is one which the court finds to be based primarily on disclosures of specific information (other than information provided by the person bringing the action) relating to allegations or transactions in a criminal, civil, or administrative hearing, in a congressional, administrative, or Government Accounting Office report, hearing, audit, or investigation, or from the news media, the court may award such sums as it considers appropriate, but in no case more than 10 percent of the proceeds, taking into account the significance of the information and the role of the person bringing the action in advancing the case to litigation. Any payment to a person under the first or second sentence of this paragraph shall be made from the proceeds. Any such person shall also receive an amount for reasonable expenses which the court finds to have been necessarily incurred, plus reasonable attorneys' fees and costs. All such expenses, fees, and costs shall be awarded against the defendant.

(2) If the Government does not proceed with an action under this section, the person bringing the action or settling the claim shall receive an amount which the court decides is reasonable for collecting the civil penalty and damages. The amount shall be not less than 25 percent and not more than 30 percent of the proceeds of the action or settlement and shall be paid out of such proceeds. Such person shall also receive an amount for reasonable expenses which the court finds to have been necessarily incurred, plus reasonable attorneys' fees and costs. All such expenses, fees, and costs shall be awarded against the defendant.

(3) Whether or not the Government proceeds with the action, if the court finds that the action was brought by a person who planned and initiated the violation of section 3729 upon which the action was brought, then the court may, to the extent the court considers appropriate, reduce the share of the proceeds of the action which the person would otherwise receive under paragraph (1) or (2) of this subsection, taking into account the role of that person in advancing the case to litigation and any relevant circumstances pertaining to the violation. If the person bringing the action is convicted of criminal conduct arising from his or her role in the violation of section 3729, that person shall be dismissed from the civil action and shall not receive any share of the proceeds of the action. Such dismissal shall not prejudice the right of the United States to continue the action, represented by the Department of Justice.

(4) If the Government does not proceed with the action and the person bringing the action conducts the action, the court may award to the defendant its reasonable attorneys' fees and expenses if the defendant prevails in the action and the court finds that the claim of the person bringing the action was clearly frivolous, clearly vexatious, or brought primarily for purposes of harassment.

(e) Certain Actions Barred.—

(1) No court shall have jurisdiction over an action brought by a former or present member of the armed forces under subsection (b) of this section against a member of the armed forces arising out of such person's service in the armed forces.

(2)

(A) No court shall have jurisdiction over an action brought under subsection (b) against a Member of Congress, a member of the judiciary, or a senior executive branch official if the action is based on evidence or information known to the Government when the action was brought.

(B) For purposes of this paragraph, "senior executive branch official" means any officer or employee listed in paragraphs (1) through (8) of section 101(f) of the Ethics in Government Act of 1978 (5 U.S.C. App.).

(3) In no event may a person bring an action under subsection (b) which is based upon allegations or transactions which are the subject of a civil suit or an administrative civil money penalty proceeding in which the Government is already a party.

(4)

(A) The court shall dismiss an action or claim under this section, unless opposed by the Government, if substantially the same allegations or transactions as alleged in the action or claim were publicly disclosed—
   (i)   in a Federal criminal, civil, or administrative hearing in which the Government or its agent is a party;
   (ii) in a congressional, Government Accountability Office, or other Federal report, hearing, audit, or investigation; or
   (iii) from the news media, unless the action is brought by the Attorney General or the person bringing the action is an original source of the information.

(B) For purposes of this paragraph, "original source" means an individual who either (i) prior to a public disclosure under subsection (e)(4)(a), has voluntarily disclosed to the Government the information on which allegations or transactions in a claim are based, or (2) who has knowledge that is independent of and materially adds to the publicly disclosed allegations or transactions, and who has voluntarily provided the information to the Government before filing an action under this section.

. . .

(h) Relief from Retaliatory Actions.—

(1) In general.—

Any employee, contractor, or agent shall be entitled to all relief necessary to make that employee, contractor, or agent whole, if that employee, contractor, or agent is discharged, demoted, suspended, threatened, harassed, or in any other manner discriminated against in the terms and conditions of employment because of lawful acts done by the employee, contractor, agent or associated others in furtherance of an action under this section or other efforts to stop 1 or more violations of this subchapter.

> (2) Relief.—
>
> Relief under paragraph (1) shall include reinstatement with the same seniority status that employee, contractor, or agent would have had but for the discrimination, 2 times the amount of back pay, interest on the back pay, and compensation for any special damages sustained as a result of the discrimination, including litigation costs and reasonable attorneys' fees. An action under this subsection may be brought in the appropriate district court of the United States for the relief provided in this subsection.
>
> (3) Limitation on bringing civil action.—
>
> A civil action under this subsection may not be brought more than 3 years after the date when the retaliation occurred.

attorneys general that forgave private loans for about 80,000 former EDMC students. Those loans were valued at close to $102.8 million (Saul, 2015).

Students could apply to have their federal loans wiped out. The fact that the settlement did not require EDMC to acknowledge wrongdoing could make it more difficult for students to prove that they were defrauded, a necessary element in seeking to have their federal student loans forgiven under Department of Education rules.

REFERENCES

Complaint for Civil Penalties, Permanent Injunction, and Other Equitable Relief. (2013). California v. Heald College, LLC., et al., 13–534793. San Francisco County Superior Court. October 10.

DOJ OPA (Department of Justice, Office of Public Affairs). (2009). "University of Phoenix Settles False Claims Act Lawsuit for $67.5 Million." United States Department of Justice. December 15. https://www.justice.gov/opa/pr/university-phoenix-settles-false-claims-act-lawsuit-675-million.

DOJ OPA (Department of Justice, Office of Public Affairs). (2015). "For-Profit Education Company to Pay $13 Million to Resolve Several Cases Alleging Submission of False Claims for Federal Student Aid." United States Department of Justice. June 24. https://www.justice.gov/opa/pr/profit-education-company-pay-13-million-resolve-several-cases-alleging-submission-false.

Douglas-Gabriel, D. (2015). "Embattled For-Profit Corinthian Colleges Closes Its Doors." *Washington Post,* April 26. https://www.washingtonpost.com/news

/business/wp/2015/04/26/embattled-for-profit-corinthian-colleges-closes-its-doors/.

Douglas-Gabriel, D. (2018). "Feds to Forgive Loans for Thousands of Students Whose Colleges Closed." *Washington Post,* December 14. https://www.washingtonpost.com/education/2018/12/14/feds-forgive-loans-thousands-students-whose-colleges-closed/.

Eder, S., and J. Medina. (2017). "Trump University Suit Settlement Approved by Judge." *New York Times,* April 1, sec. A, p. 16.

FTC. (2016). "DeVry University Agrees to $100 Million Settlement with FTC." Federal Trade Commission. December 15. https://www.ftc.gov/news-events/press-releases/2016/12/devry-university-agrees-100-million-settlement-ftc.

HELP Committee (Health, Education, Labor and Pensions Committee). (2012). "For Profit Higher Education: The Failure to Safeguard the Federal Investment and Ensure Student Success: Majority Committee Staff Report and Accompanying Minority Committee Staff Views." United States Senate, Health, Education, Labor and Pensions Committee. July 30. https://www.help.senate.gov/imo/media/for_profit_report/PartI.pdf.

Joint Complaint. (2011). United States, et al. v. Education Management Corp., et al., 07-cv-00461-TFM. W. Dist. Pennsylvania. Joint Complaint in Intervention by the United States of America, and the States of California, Florida, Illinois, and Indiana. August 8.

Leys, T. (2015). "Ex-ISU Scientist Sentenced to 57 Months in Prison" *Des Moines Register,* July 1. https://www.desmoinesregister.com/story/news/crime-and-courts/2015/07/01/dong-pyou-han-sentencing-iowa-state-scientist-aids-vaccine-fraud-case/29560297/.

Lynch, L. (2015). "Attorney General Loretta E. Lynch Delivers Remarks at Press Conference Announcing $95.5 Million Settlement with For-Profit College Company." United States Justice Department, Office of Public Affairs. November 16. https://www.justice.gov/opa/speech/attorney-general-loretta-e-lynch-delivers-remarks-press-conference-announcing-955-million.

Lynch News Conference. (2015). C-SPAN Video Library. November 16. https://www.c-span.org/video/?400827-1/attorney-general-loretta-lynch-news-conference.

Saul, S. (2015). "For-Profit College System Expected to Pay Millions." *New York Times,* November 16. https://www.nytimes.com/2015/11/16/us/for-profit-college-system-expected-to-pay-millions.html.

Taylor, K. (2020). "Lori Loughlin and Mossimo Giannulli Get Prison in College Admissions Case." *New York Times,* August 21. https://www.nytimes.com/2020/08/21/us/lori-loughlin-mossimo-giannulli-sentencing.html.

Warren, E., R. Durbin, and R. Blumenthal. (2015). Letter to Arne Duncan and Loretta Lynch. *Elizabeth Warren, United States Senator for Massachusetts.* November 30. https://www.warren.senate.gov/files/documents/2015-11-30_Letter_to_Depts_of_Edu_and_Justice_re_EDMC_Settlement.pdf.

TWELVE

False Advertising

DOES RED BULL ACTUALLY GIVE YOU WINGS? The energy drink company's whimsical ads surely wouldn't be considered anything other than hyperbole, right? In 2014, a group of consumers challenged that marketing slogan, though not for its literal meaning (O'Reilly, 2014). Rather, the plaintiffs in this class-action lawsuit alleged that Red Bull's claims that the drink improved concentration and reaction speeds wasn't backed by scientific proof. The plaintiffs claimed that Red Bull's marketing was not puffery—harmless exaggerations—but was deceptive and fraudulent and therefore violated laws against false advertising. The company denied any wrongdoing and maintained that its marketing had always been truthful and accurate. However, to avoid litigation costs, Red Bull settled the lawsuit, agreeing to pay $6.5 million to reimburse disappointed consumers $10 or give them a $15 voucher for more Red Bull.

Consumers expect a certain amount of exaggeration in advertising. *This lipstick is the best. That cookie tastes better than all others. You'll never find a car that is as fine an automobile as this one.* But when does this sort of puffery cross the line into deception? That's a question that consumer protection agencies study closely.

The Federal Trade Commission (FTC) enforces federal laws prohibiting false or misleading information in advertisements and marketing. Under the Federal Trade Commission Act, advertisements must be truthful and non-deceptive, be backed by evidence, and cannot be unfair (15 U.S.C. § 55). The FTC's mission is to protect consumers and competition by preventing anti-competitive, deceptive, and unfair business practices. Cases concerning false advertisements are brought in civil lawsuits, not criminal. Corporate

STATUTES

15 U.S.C. § 52. Dissemination of False Advertisements

(a) Unlawfulness

It shall be unlawful for any person, partnership, or corporation to disseminate, or cause to be disseminated, any false advertisement—

(1) By United States mails, or in or having an effect upon commerce, by any means, for the purpose of inducing, or which is likely to induce, directly or indirectly the purchase of food, drugs, devices, services, or cosmetics; or

(2) By any means, for the purpose of inducing, or which is likely to induce, directly or indirectly, the purchase in or having an effect upon commerce, of food, drugs, devices, services, or cosmetics.

(b) Unfair or deceptive act or practice
The dissemination or the causing to be disseminated of any false advertisement within the provisions of subsection (a) of this section shall be an unfair or deceptive act or practice in or affecting commerce within the meaning of section 45 of this title.

15 U.S.C. § 55. Additional Definitions

For the purposes of sections 52 to 54 of this title—

(a) False advertisement

(1) The term "false advertisement" means an advertisement, other than labeling, which is misleading in a material respect; and in determining whether any advertisement is misleading, there shall be taken into account (among other things) not only representations made or suggested by statement, word, design, device, sound, or any combination thereof, but also the extent to which the advertisement fails to reveal facts material in the light of such representations or material with respect to consequences which may result from the use of the commodity to which the advertisement relates under the conditions prescribed in said advertisement, or under such conditions as are customary or usual. No advertisement of a drug shall be deemed to be false if it is disseminated only to members of the medical profession, contains no false representation of a material fact, and includes, or is accompanied in each instance by truthful disclosure of, the formula showing quantitatively each ingredient of such drug.

defendants can be fined and can be enjoined by court order from activities or statements that are deceptive, and the companies can be put under compliance monitoring for a period of time. Any fines collected on civil actions are usually used for consumer refunds.

States, too, have consumer protection laws that they enforce to ensure that customers are not duped by bad information into buying products or services. Misleading promotions may include bait-and-switch practices, whereby the seller promises a bargain on an item to lure consumers to a store but, when they arrive, the item doesn't exist or there is only a limited number available. Deceptive practices also include advertising false "going out of business" sales, misrepresenting a used item as new, and misleading the buyer about the country of origin where a product was made.

In the civil lawsuits brought by the FTC in the cases studied in this chapter, the issue is again that line between promotion and deception.

MAGIC SHOES

In the mid-2000s, a new trend in footwear gained traction. Promoted as a way to get in shape and lose weight with no more effort than tying your shoelaces, "toning" shoes quickly grew to a $1 billion per year niche in the athletic shoe industry. While most athletic shoes are designed to give the wearer support and stability, toning shoes did the opposite. The theory was that a slight instability built into the shoe forced muscles to work harder, resulting in weight loss and muscle toning, shaping, and strengthening (Skechers Complaint, 2012).

Several companies sold toning footwear products, but the most popular brands were Skechers and Reebok. Marketing materials told consumers that they could "get in shape without setting foot in a gym" (Skechers Complaint, 2012, Exhibit 1) and that the shoes would deliver "up to 28% more of a workout for your butt . . . [a]nd up to 11 percent more for your hamstrings and calves" (Reebok Complaint, 2012, Exhibit 8). For only $100 a pair, consumers could get "a better butt and better legs with every step" (Reebok Complaint, 2012, Exhibit 11).

The marketing materials and advertisements featured celebrities such as retired NFL player Joe Montana and celebrities such as Kim Kardashian and Brooke Burke, who each promoted Skechers brand shoes. Kardashian's ad, in which she fired her personal trainer in favor of her toning shoes, was unveiled during the 2011 Super Bowl. Burke's ads promised that the shoes would improve the wearer's posture, legs, and core and boasted that "the newest way to burn calories and tone and strengthen muscles was to tie their Shape Up shoelaces" (Skechers Complaint, 2012, p. 5). Reebok's advertisements touted a study implying there was science behind the improved fitness consumers could expect as the shoes heightened the effectiveness of their workouts by precise percentage increases. The FTC claimed that these studies were unsubstantiated and did not prove any benefit.

In truth, none of the ads could be supported by science. The theory that unstable running shoes would be a benefit had not been scientifically tested, despite studies by a California chiropractor that Skechers offered as proof. The doctor recommended the products based on the results of his own "independent" studies that tested the shoes' benefits compared to other, regular athletic shoes (Skechers Complaint, 2012, p. 7). The doctor claimed that wearers lost 2.78 pounds, compared to 0.30 pounds for the control group; reduced body fat by 1.31 percent, compared to 0.57 percent for the control subjects; saw a 114 percent improvement in muscle development in the glutei, hamstring, and gastrocnemius (the main calf muscle), versus a 68 percent increase in the control group; and had a 23 percent improvement in low-back endurance strength, while the control group saw only 0.04 percent improvement.

The FTC claimed Skechers' studies were flawed. The weight loss study was six weeks long, had eight participants, and did not have a control group of participants who wore standard athletic shoes. The doctor's second study was backed by data that had been altered and was incomplete. Some participants who gained weight wearing the Skechers shoes were recorded as having lost weight. Many of that study's subjects were connected to the researchers, including the spouses of two of the study's coauthors, the parents of one coauthor, and employees of the chiropractor. The ads carrying the chiropractor's endorsement did not disclose that he was compensated to endorse the product or that he was married to a Skechers senior vice president.

In fact, the rocker-bottom design could actually result in injuries. As noted in *Consumer Reports*, the shoes were supposed to promote instability, which might also lead to turned ankles, falls, and other injuries (Mays, 2011). The Consumer Product Safety Commission received dozens of complaints of injuries, ranging from tendonitis and pain in the foot, leg, and hip, to broken bones, some requiring surgery.

"Skechers' unfounded claims went beyond stronger and more toned muscles. The company even made claims about weight loss and cardiovascular health," said David Vladeck, director of the FTC's Bureau of Consumer Protection. "The FTC's message, for Skechers and other national advertisers, is to shape up your substantiation or tone down your claims" (FTC, May 16, 2012).

RESOLUTION

In September 2011, the FTC settled its complaint against Reebok, with the company agreeing to pay $25 million and to stop marketing its EasyTone and RunTone footwear with deceptive ads. In May 2012, Skechers U.S.A. agreed to pay $40 million and to stop promoting toning shoes, such as Resistance Runner, Toners, and Tone Ups, with deceptive advertisements. In addition, Skechers settled a state claim for $5 million and agreed to pay $5 million in class-action legal fees.

At the same time, Skechers representatives denied any deception and stressed that the company settled only to avoid the cost and distraction of litigation. "The company has received overwhelmingly enthusiastic feedback from literally thousands of customers who have tried our toning shoes for themselves and have written unsolicited testimonials about their positive experiences," Skechers president Michael Greenberg told the *Los Angeles Times* (Puzzanghera, 2012).

Both companies were barred from making claims about the supposed muscle-strengthening, weight loss, or other health- or fitness-related benefits of their toning shoes, unless backed by scientific evidence.

In 2012, another athletic shoe company, New Balance, settled a class-action lawsuit filed in a Massachusetts state court. The three women who initiated the lawsuit alleged that the company's ads promised that its TrueBalance and Rock&Tone toning shoes were a "hidden beauty secret" that would help consumers burn 8 percent more calories than regular shoes, and that the shoe "activated" lower body muscles (Hines, 2012). New Balance agreed to pay $2.3 million to refund consumers $100 per pair of toning shoes they had purchased. The settlement also prohibited the company from claiming that its shoes promote health without proof from clinical studies. The FTC was not involved in the New Balance case.

Skechers and Reebok customers could submit a claim with the FTC for their refunds. In August 2012, the FTC sent approximately 315,000 checks to Reebok customers (FTC, 2013), and a year later, the commission sent more than 509,000 checks to Skechers customers (FTC, 2013).

FTC. (2011). "Reebok to Pay $25 Million in Customer Refunds to Settle FTC Charges of Deceptive Advertising of EasyTone and RunTone Shoes." Federal Trade Commission. September 28. https://www.ftc.gov/news-events/press-releases/2011/09/reebok-pay-25-million-customer-refunds-settle-ftc-charges.

FTC. (May 16, 2012). "Skechers Will Pay $40 Million to Settle FTC Charges That It Deceived Consumers with Ads for 'Toning Shoes.'" Federal Trade Commission. https://www.ftc.gov/news-events/press-releases/2012/05/skechers-will-pay-40-million-settle-ftc-charges-it-deceived.

FTC. (August 7, 2012). "Refunds Stemming from Reebok's Settlement with FTC Mailed to Consumers Who Bought EasyTone and RunTone Shoes and EasyTone Apparel." Federal Trade Commission. https://www.ftc.gov/news-events/press-releases/2012/08/refunds-stemming-reeboks-settlement-ftc-mailed-consumers-who.

FTC. (2013). "FTC Mails Refund Checks to Consumers Who Bought Skechers' Shape-Ups and Other 'Toning' Shoes." Federal Trade Commission. July 11. https://www.ftc.gov/news-events/press-releases/2013/07/ftc-mails-refund-checks-consumers-who-bought-skechers-shape-ups.

Hines, A. (2012). "New Balance Pays Fat Settlement in Toning Shoes Lawsuit to People It Did Not Slim." *Huffington Post,* August 29. https://www.huffpost.com/entry/new-balance-toning-shoe-settlement_n_1839537.

Mays, D. (2011). "Are Toning Shoes Unsafe? Reports of Injuries Raise Concerns." *Consumer Reports.* May 25. https://www.consumerreports.org/cro/news/2011/05/are-toning-shoes-unsafe-reports-of-injuries-raise-concern/index.htm.

O'Reilly, L. (2014). "Red Bull Will Pay $10 to Customers Disappointed the Drink Didn't Actually Give Them 'Wings.'" *Business Insider,* October 8. https://www.businessinsider.com/red-bull-settles-false-advertising-lawsuit-for-13-million-2014-10.

Puzzanghera, J. 2012. Skechers agrees to pay $50 million to settle toning-shoe cases. *Los Angeles Times,* May 17. https://www.latimes.com/business/la-xpm-2012-may-17-la-fi-ftc-skechers-20120517-story.html.

Reebok Complaint. (2012). Federal Trade Commission v. Reebok International, Ltd., 11-cv-02046. N. Dist. Ohio. Complaint for Permanent Injunction and Other Equitable Relief. September 28.

Skechers Complaint. (2012). Federal Trade Commission v. Skechers U.S.A., Inc., 12-cv-01214. N. Dist. Ohio. Complaint for Permanent Injunction and Other Equitable Relief. May 16.

INDEX

Note: Page numbers followed by *b* and *f* indicate text boxes and figures, respectively.

brokerages, Ponzi schemes at, 36
Brown-Mackie College, 152
Budovsky, Arthur, 93–100
Bureau of Alcohol, Tobacco, Firearms, and
  Explosives, 108
Burke, Brooke, 170–71

Caldwell, Leslie R., 97
California, mortgage fraud in, 18
Callihan, Charles, 110–11, 114–15
Camp Minden, munitions explosion at,
  106–15
carders, 63, 74, 92. *See also* credit card fraud
carding, 63
cars: loans for, 38–39; product defects in,
  77–89
Centers for Medicare and Medicaid Services, 59
certificates of destruction (COD), 107
charges, criminal, 2–3; in corporate crime
  cases, 85; in cybercrime cases, 64–65; in
  embezzlement cases, 10–11; in environmental cases, 109, 110–11; in health care
  fraud cases, 54–55, 58*b;* in insider-trading cases, 140–41; in money laundering
  cases, 97; in mortgage fraud cases, 24; in
  Ponzi schemes, 40
Children's Health Insurance Program
  (CHIP), 59
China, Avon in, 125–35
CHIP. *See* Children's Health Insurance
  Program
Chukharev, Maxim, 97
Church of Jesus Christ of Latter-day Saints
  (LDS), 37*b*, 38, 39
civil lawsuits: against corporations, 87;
  under False Claims Act, 152; under
  Foreign Corrupt Practices Act, 120; in
  insider-trading cases, 144, 145; over false
  advertising, 168–70
Clark, John Scott, 37*b*–38*b*
Clean Water Act, 105
COD. *See* certificates of destruction
college admissions, 150–58
community mental health centers, 52–54
conduct, relevant, 12–13
Congress, US, response to Great Recession,
  18. *See also specific laws*

conspiracy statutes, 19, 25*b*
Consumer Product Safety Commission,
  171
consumer protection laws, 168, 170
Consumer Reports, 171
convertible virtual currencies (CVCs), 103
Cook, Julian Abele, Jr., 30–31
cooperation, as consideration in sentencing,
  24–29
Corinthian Colleges, 158
corporate crime, 77–89; civil lawsuits based
  on, 87; investigations of, 77, 85–86;
  Justice Manual on, 77, 78*b*–79*b;* prosecution of, 77–79, 78*b*–79*b*, 85–89; US
  Sentencing Guidelines on, 132*b*–34*b.*
  See also bribery
corporations, vs. individuals, prosecution
  of, 3, 77, 88–89, 133–35
corruption, in foreign bribery, 119–20,
  121*b*–22*b*
Costa Rica, money laundering in, 93–96
Countrywide, 19
court proceedings, 2–3. *See also* prosecution; sentencing
credit card fraud, 62–73, 92
Cressey, Donald, 5–6
criminal charges. *See* charges
cryptocurrency, 92
Cubero, Marco, 96
currency, digital, in money laundering,
  92–94, 95*f,* 100–103
CVCs. *See* convertible virtual currencies
cybercrime, 62–75; forms and tactics of,
  62–66; future of, 73–75; investigations
  of, 62–65, 75; money laundering in,
  92–94; prosecution of, 62, 66–70;
  sentencing for, 70–73; statutes on,
  68*b*–69*b*

Dark Web, 74
DEA. *See* Drug Enforcement Agency
debit card fraud, 73, 92
Defense, US Department of, 108, 110
defense contractors, foreign bribery by, 118
deferred prosecution agreements (DPAs):
  in corporate liability cases, 77, 85–89;
  critics of, 77, 87–89; definition of, 77; in
  foreign bribery cases, 130, 131

detention, pending trial, 55–56
DeVos, Betsy, 158
DeVry University, 151*b*
DeYoung, Curtis, 37*b*
Digene Corp., 139
digital currency, in money laundering, 92–94, 95*f*, 100–103
discretion, of prosecutors, 3
DOE. *See* Education, US Department of
DOJ. *See* Justice, US Department of
domestic concerns, 119, 120
DPAs. *See* deferred prosecution agreements
Drug Enforcement Agency (DEA), 50
Duke, Ronnie, 20–33. *See also United States v. Ronnie Duke*
dump shops, 63–66
Duncan, Arne, 157
Dunn, David, 63, 64, 67
Durbin, Richard J., 157–58

EA. *See* Education Affiliates
EDMC. *See* Education Management Corporation
Education, US Department of (DOE), 153, 157, 158, 166
Education Affiliates (EA), 151*b*
Education Management Corporation (EDMC), 152–66; federal funds received by, 152–53; student loans at, 157–66; student recruitment by, 153–58. *See also United States, et al. v. Education Management Corp.*
E-Gold, 92–93, 98
El Amine, Azzeddine, 97
email accounts, in cybercrime, 64
embezzlement, 5–15; collateral costs of, 5, 6, 10, 13–14; definition of, 5; estimated losses from, 5, 6, 12; Fraud Triangle of, 5–6; investigations of, 8–10; motivations for, 2, 6; prevalence of, 5, 6; prosecution of, 10–13; sentencing for, 11–14
employees, theft by. *See* embezzlement
end use certifications (EUCs), 107, 111, 112
environmental crimes, 105–15; categories of harm from, 105–6; forms of, 105; investigations of, 107, 110; prosecution of, 109, 110–15; sentencing for, 109, 111–12

environmental laws, EPA in enforcement of, 105
Environmental Protection Agency (EPA), 105–11; Criminal Investigation Division of, 110–11; establishment of, 105; hazardous waste under, 108; in munitions explosion case, 106–11; purpose of, 105
EPA. *See* Environmental Protection Agency
Erbitux, 137
Erickson, Gene, 82
escape attempts, statutes on, 26*b*, 31
escrow companies, 17, 20
EUCs. *See* end use certifications
evidence: in cybercrime cases, 66–70; exculpatory, 29n1
exculpatory evidence, 29n1
explosions, munitions, at Camp Minden, 106–15
Explo Systems, 106–15

FAFSA. *See* Free Application for Federal Student Aid
false advertising, 168–72, 169*b*
False Claims Act: academic fraud cases under, 151*b*, 152, 154, 157; excerpts of text of, 159*b*–66*b*
FBI. *See* Federal Bureau of Investigation
FCPA. *See* Foreign Corrupt Practices Act
FDA. *See* Food and Drug Administration
FDIC. *See* Federal Deposit Insurance Corporation
Federal Bureau of Investigation (FBI): in academic fraud cases, 150; in corporate crime cases, 85; on embezzlement, definition of, 5; in embezzlement cases, 9; in environmental cases, 110; in health care fraud cases, 50, 58; in mortgage fraud cases, 20, 23, 30
Federal Deposit Insurance Corporation (FDIC), 19
Federal Direct Loan Program, 152–53
Federal Family Education Loan Program (FFELP), 152–53
Federal Rules of Criminal Procedure, 24–27, 27*b*
Federal Supplemental Educational Opportunity grants, 153

Horizon Notes, 38, 40, 44–45
HSI. *See* Homeland Security Investigations
HUD-1 forms, 20
Huffman, Felicity, 150
HYIPs. *See* high-yield investment programs

ICE. *See* Immigration and Customs Enforcement
Idexx Laboratories Inc., 139–40
ignition switches, faulty, 77–85
ImClone, 137
Immigration and Customs Enforcement (ICE), 96
incentives, in student recruitment, 151*b*, 153, 155
Independent Commercial Lending, 38
Independent Financial and Investment, 39
Independent Property Management, 38
individuals, vs. corporations, prosecution of, 3, 77, 88–89, 133–35
insider trading, 137–48; forms and tactics of, 137–40; investigations of, 145; prosecution of, 140–45; sentencing for, 141–45, 142*b*–44*b*; victims in, 138, 141
interest rates: mortgage, 19; student loan, 156
Internal Revenue Service (IRS): in embezzlement cases, 7–10, 14–15; in health care fraud cases, 50; in money laundering cases, 96
investigations, 2; of academic fraud, 150, 156; of corporate crime, 77, 85–86; of cybercrime, 62–65, 75; of embezzlement, 8–10; of environmental crimes, 107, 110; of foreign bribery, 118, 128–34; of health care fraud, 50–52, 54; of insider trading, 145; of money laundering, 96; of mortgage fraud, 20, 23–24; of Ponzi schemes, 40, 47–48
investments. *See* insider trading; Ponzi schemes
IRS. *See* Internal Revenue Service
issuers, 119, 120

Jackson, Douglas, 93
Jefferson, Thomas, 121*b*
Jindal, Bobby, 115

JMC. *See* Joint Munitions Command
Johnson, Donald. *See United States v. Donald Johnson*
Joint Munitions Command (JMC), 107, 111, 112
Jones, Richard A., 72
Joseph, David C., 109
jurisdiction, 3
Justice, US Department of (DOJ): in academic fraud cases, 151*b*, 154, 157, 158; in corporate crime cases, 77, 78*b*–79*b*, 88; in foreign bribery cases, 118, 120, 121*b*–25*b*, 130–35; in insider-trading cases, 140–41; in response to Great Recession, 18
Justice Manual, 77, 78*b*–79*b*

Kardashian, Kim, 170–71
Kats, Vladimir, 93–94, 97–99
Kelley, Andrew Dean, 37*b*
Key Worldwide Foundation, 150
kickbacks, in health care fraud, 50, 52, 53, 55, 57
know your customer (KYC) procedures, 91, 95
Koons, Lionel, 109, 110–14
KYC. *See* know your customer

Lampkin, Kenneth, 110–12
Landrieu, Mary, 110
larceny, embezzlement as category of, 5
laws. *See* statutes; *specific laws*
LDS. *See* Church of Jesus Christ of Latter-day Saints
liability, corporate. *See* corporate crime
Liberty Reserve, 70, 92–100, 95*f*. *See also United States v. Liberty Reserve*
Litecoin, 92
loans: automobile, 38–39; mortgage, 17–20 (*See also* mortgage fraud); student (*See* student loans)
Los Angeles Times (newspaper), 172
Loughlin, Lori, 150–52
Louisiana, munitions explosion in, 106–15
Louisiana State Police, 106, 108, 110, 111, 115
lulling behavior, 47–48
Lynch, Loretta E., 157
Lyons, Chip, 39, 44–48

Madoff, Bernie, 1, 35–36
Mahoney, Michael T., 154
mail fraud statutes, 19
Markey, Edward J., 87
Marmilev, Mark, 97
Marquet International, 36
Martha Stewart Living, 137
Medicaid, 50, 52, 54, 56, 59
medical claims and records, falsifying,
    50–55
Medicare, 50–59, 58*b*
Medicare Fraud Strike Force, 50–52, 54,
    57–58, 58*b*
mental health centers, community, 52–54
Michigan, mortgage fraud in, 17, 20
mitigating factors, in sentencing, 27, 72
money laundering, 91–103; in cybercrime,
    92–94; definition of, 91; digital cur-
    rency in, 92–94, 95*f,* 100–103; forms
    and tactics of, 92–96, 95*f,* 100; global
    scale of, 100; in health care fraud, 55, 56;
    investigations of, 96; prosecution of,
    96–100; sentencing for, 98–100; stat-
    utes on, 91–92, 101*b–3b;* steps in, 91
Money Laundering Control Act of 1986,
    91–92
Montana, Joe, 170
mortgage fraud, 17–33; ghost loans in, 17,
    20–24; investigations of, 20, 23–24;
    prosecution of, 18, 24–27; sentencing
    for, 24–31; statistics on cases of, 19;
    statutes used for, 19, 24, 25*b;* straw
    buyers in, 17, 18, 21–24
Mortgage Fraud Working Group, 18
mortgage industry: lending practices in,
    17–20; non-bank lenders in, 19
motivations, 2, 6
M6 propellant, 106–8, 111
munitions explosions, at Camp Minden,
    106–15
Murphy, Stephen J., 32–33

NASDAQ, 138–40, 144
National Health Care Anti-fraud Associa-
    tion, 58
National Highway Traffic Safety Adminis-
    tration (NHTSA), 80–85
Nebbia condition, 56

New Balance, 172
NHTSA. *See* National Highway Traffic
    Safety Administration
Nixon, Richard, 105
nonprosecution agreements (NPAs), 77, 131
Novastar, 19
NPAs. *See* nonprosecution agreements

Obama, Barack, 18
Obermiller, Cheryl, 7–15
Obermiller Construction Services, 6–15
Occupational Safety and Health Adminis-
    tration (OSHA), 108, 111
OECD. *See* Organization for Economic
    Cooperation and Development
O'Hear, Michael M., 105–6
oil companies, foreign bribery by, 118
Operation Varsity Blues, 150–52
opportunity, in embezzlement, 6
Organization for Economic Cooperation
    and Development (OECD), 119, 121*b*
OSHA. *See* Occupational Safety and
    Health Administration

PACER filing system, 67
parsimony clause, 72, 74*b*
partial hospitalization program (PHP),
    52–54
Patient Protection and Affordable Care Act
    (ACA), 59
PCN. *See* Psychiatric Consulting Network
Pell Grants, 152–53
Perkins loans, 153
PHP. *See* partial hospitalization program
plagiarism, 152
plea agreements: binding, 24–27; definition
    of, 13; in embezzlement cases, 11–13; in
    environmental crimes, 109; Federal
    Rules of Criminal Procedure on, 24–27,
    27*b;* in health care fraud cases, 56; in
    money laundering cases, 97–98; in
    mortgage fraud cases, 24–27; in Ponzi
    schemes, 46; in sentencing, 13, 24–27
point-of-sale systems, 62–63, 67
Ponzi, Charles, 35
Ponzi schemes, 35–48; definition of, 35;
    famous cases of, 35–36; forms and
    tactics of, 36–40; high-yield investment

programs as, 93; investigations of, 40, 47–48; prosecution of, 40–46; sentencing in, 46–47; statute of limitations and, 47–48; in Utah, 36, 37b–38b
Postal Inspection Service, 140
pressure, as motivation for embezzlement, 6
private-placement memoranda, 39, 45
private placement offerings, 39
Procare Management and Financial Network, 53
product defects, 77–89
product recalls, 82, 84–87
prosecution, 2–3; of corporate crime, 77–79, 78b–79b, 85–89; of corporations vs. individuals, 3, 77, 88–89, 133–35; of cybercrime, 62, 66–70; discretion in, 3; of embezzlement, 10–13; of environmental crimes, 109, 110–15; of foreign bribery, 119–20; of health care fraud, 54–56, 58b; of insider trading, 140–45; of money laundering, 96–100; of mortgage fraud, 18, 24–27; of Ponzi schemes, 40–46; strategies of, 3
Psychiatric Consulting Network (PCN), 53, 55, 56

qui tam lawsuits, 153–54, 157, 161b–64b

Randall, Dee Allen, 36, 38–48. See also Utah v. Dee Randall
RCRA. See Resource Conservation and Recovery Act
RDAP. See Residential Drug Abuse Program
reactive waste, 108
recalls, product, 82, 84–87
Red Bull, 168
Reebok, 170–72
registry, white-collar crime, 36, 46, 48
regulators, statutes on making false statements to, 85, 86b. See also specific agencies
relevant conduct, 12–13
research fraud, 150, 152
Residential Drug Abuse Program (RDAP), 30
Resource Conservation and Recovery Act (RCRA), 105, 108, 109–10

Richet, Jean-Loup, 93
Rosenstein, Rod, 88, 121b–25b, 135
Rousseau, Roger, 55, 57
Russia, cybercrime in, 63, 66, 73

Schlotsky's Deli, 62–63
SDM. See sensing diagnostic module
SEC. See Securities and Exchange Commission
Secret Service, US: in cybercrime cases, 63–66, 73; Electronic Crimes Task Force of, 63; in money laundering cases, 96
Securities and Exchange Commission (SEC): in foreign bribery cases, 118–20, 130–31; in insider-trading cases, 140, 144, 145
securities fraud, statutes on, 140, 146b–48b. See also insider trading; Ponzi schemes
Seleznev, Roman, 63–75. See also United States v. Roman Seleznev
self-reporting, of foreign bribery, 120, 130
Senate Committee on Health, Education, Labor, and Pensions (HELP Committee), 156–57
sensing diagnostic module (SDM), 81–82
sentencing, 3–4; aggravating factors in, 27, 71, 72, 141; cooperation as consideration in, 24–29; of corporations vs. individuals, 3, 77, 88–89; for cybercrime, 70–73; for embezzlement, 11–14; for environmental crimes, 109, 111–12; for health care fraud, 56–57; for insider trading, 141–45, 142b–44b; mitigating factors in, 27, 72; for money laundering, 98–100; for mortgage fraud, 24–31; plea agreements in, 13, 24–27; for Ponzi schemes, 46–47; victims as consideration in, 3. See also United States Sentencing Guidelines
servers, in cybercrime, 64, 66
Sessions, Jeff, 122b
Shadowcrew, 92
Shearman & Sterling, 131
shoes, toning, 170–72
short-selling, 139–40
Singer, William "Rick," 150

Skechers, 170–72
Smith, David, 107, 109–12, 115
South University, 152
Stafford loans, 153, 156
statutes. *See specific laws and subjects*
statutes of limitations, for fraud, 47–48
Stewart, Martha, 1, 137
Stop Fraud Utah, 36
straw buyers, in mortgage fraud, 17, 18,
   21–24
Stroud, A.M., 114
structuring deposits, 91
student loans, 156–66; default rates on, 153,
   156–57; at Education Management
   Corporation, 157–66; forgiveness of,
   158, 166; types of, 152–53
student recruitment, 151*b*, 153–58
subprime loans: for cars, 38; for houses,
   17–18
Superintendencia General de Entidades
   Financieras (SUGEF), 94–96
Supreme Court, US: on exculpatory evidence, 29n1; on US Sentencing Guidelines, 12
surgery, health care fraud in, 50

title searches, 20
TNT, 107, 108, 115
toning footwear, 170–72
Toyota, 87
Transportation, US Department of, 110
Treasury, US Department of, 92, 96
Trump, Donald, 151*b*, 158
Trump University, 151*b*
trust, abuse of, 140–45, 143*b*
Tyvaso, 139

Union Central Life Insurance, 38
United Nations Office on Drugs and
   Crime (UNODC), 93, 100
*United States, et al. v. Education Manage-
   ment Corp., et al.,* 150–66; facts of case,
   152–55; resolution of, 157–66
*United States Code. See specific laws and
   subjects*
United States Sentencing Guidelines
   (USSG): as advisory vs. mandatory, 12;
   aggravating factors in, 27, 71, 72, 141; on

bank fraud, 11–13; calculations of sentencing range using, 27–28; cooperation
   as consideration in, 24; on corporations,
   132*b*–34*b*; in cybercrime cases, 70–71;
   establishment of, 12; in insider-trading
   cases, 141, 142*b*–44*b*, 144; mitigating
   factors in, 27, 72; in money laundering
   cases, 98; in mortgage fraud cases, 28;
   victims as consideration in, 3; on wire
   fraud, 28
United States v. Armando Gonzalez, 50–59;
   facts of case, 52–54; investigation in, 54;
   prosecution of, 54–56; sentencing in,
   56–57
*United States v. Avon Products, Inc., Avon
   Products (China) Co., Ltd.,* 118–35; facts
   of case, 125–28; investigation in, 128–34;
   resolution of, 130–35
United States v. Booker, 12
United States v. Cowell, 5–15; aftermath of,
   14–15; facts of case, 7–10; investigation
   in, 8–10; prosecution of, 10–13; resolution of, 13–14
United States v. Donald Johnson, 137–48;
   facts of case, 138–40; prosecution of,
   140–45; sentencing in, 141–45
United States v. Fincher, et al., 105–15; facts
   of case, 106–8; investigation in, 107, 110;
   prosecution of, 109, 110–15; sentencing
   in, 109, 111–12
United States v. General Motors, 77–89;
   critics of, 87–89; facts of case, 77–85;
   prosecution of, 77–79, 85–89; resolution of, 85–87
*United States v. Liberty Reserve, S.A.,
   Arthur Budovsky, et al.,* 91–103; facts of
   case, 92–96; prosecution of, 96–100;
   sentencing in, 98–100
United States v. Liebo, 119–20
United States v. Roman Seleznev, 62–75;
   facts of case, 62–66; investigation in,
   62–65; prosecution of, 62, 66–70;
   sentencing in, 70–73
United States v. Ronnie Duke, 17–33; aftermath of, 31–33; facts of case, 20–24;
   investigation in, 20, 23–24; prosecution
   of, 24–27; sentencing in, 24–31
United Support for Humanity, 98–99

United Therapeutics Corp. (UTHR), 139
University of Phoenix, 151*b*
UNODC. *See* United Nations Office on Drugs and Crime
US Attorneys' Offices: Annual Statistical Report of, 19; deferred prosecution agreements with, 85; *Justice Manual* of, 77, 78*b*–79*b*
USSG. *See* United States Sentencing Guidelines
Utah: Ponzi schemes in, 36, 37*b*–38*b*; statutes of, 40, 41*b*–44*b*; white-collar crime registry in, 36, 46, 48
Utah Division of Securities, 39–40, 45, 47
Utah v. Dee Randall, 35–48; aftermath of, 47; facts of case, 38–40; investigation in, 40; prosecution of, 40–46; sentencing in, 46–47
UTHR. *See* United Therapeutics Corp.

victims: as consideration in sentencing, 3; in insider trading, 138, 141; nonfinancial losses of, 3–4
virtual currencies, 92, 103. *See also* digital currency
Vladeck, David, 172

Wagner, Ben, 18
Waksal, Sam, 137
Wall Street Journal, 138–39
Walmart, 7

Warren, Elizabeth, 157–58
Washington, Lynntoya, 153–54
Washington Mutual, 19
waste: hazardous, 108, 111, 113*b*–14*b*; reactive, 108
Western Union, 92
whistleblowers: in academic fraud, 151*b*, 154, 157; in False Claims Act, 152, 154; in foreign bribery, 120; in insider trading, 145
white-collar crimes: court proceedings with, 2–3 (*See also* prosecution); investigations of (*See* investigations); methods and motivations in, 2; resolution of cases, 3–4 (*See also* sentencing)
WHO. *See* World Health Organization
willful blindness, 120
wire fraud: in corporate crime cases, 85; in environmental crimes, 111; in mortgage fraud cases, 19, 24, 28; sentencing for, 28; statutes on, 19, 24, 25*b*
Wojcieszek, Keith, 64
Woodwell, Keith, 40
work-study, 153
World Health Organization (WHO), 105
World Trade Organization (WTO), 125
Wright, William Terry, 109, 110–12
WTO. *See* World Trade Organization

Yassine, Ahmed, 94–95
Yates, Sally, 88